"What a fine book! Professor Lennox obviously knows whereof he speaks; he also has an enviable ability to make difficult matters crystal clear. This book is as good as it gets in the religion and science area."

—Alvin Plantinga, the Emeritus John A. O'Brien Professor
of Philosophy, University of Notre Dame

"This book is a delight to read: It is thoughtful, perceptive, friendly, and bold when it needs to be. Dr. Lennox has gone right to the heart of the matter in his thinking about Genesis and the age of the earth, and how that is a different question from purposeless evolution. In this well-written book, which shows good learning accessibly presented, Dr. Lennox has helped us to think clearly about these questions. I look forward to sharing this book with many people. Thank you, Dr. Lennox!"

—C. John Collins, Professor of Old Testament,
Covenant Theological Seminary

"This remarkable book by John Lennox is exactly what I've been looking to recommend! Its treatment of Genesis 1 and 2 in connection with modern science and ancient Near Eastern culture is accessible, wide-ranging, balanced, and irenic. Lennox has written a wise, well-informed work, and it deserves the widest readership possible."

—Paul Copan, Professor and Pledger Family Chair
of Philosophy and Ethics, Palm Beach Atlantic
University, West Palm Beach, Florida

"Dr. Lennox is an apt guide for exploring both the Bible and science. He admirably argues that they both reveal the same Creator and Designer. In this careful and well-documented study, he examines all the pertinent issues concerning the meaning of the Genesis creation account. Every careful reader will come away more knowledgeable, wiser, and better able to defend the truth of the Bible before a skeptical world."

—Doug Groothuis, Professor of Philosophy, Denver
y, and author of *Christian Apologetics*

SEVEN DAYS
THAT DIVIDE THE
WORLD

SEVEN DAYS THAT DIVIDE THE WORLD

THE BEGINNING ACCORDING TO **GENESIS** AND **SCIENCE**

JOHN C. LENNOX

ZONDERVAN.com/
AUTHORTRACKER
follow your favorite authors

We want to hear from you. Please send your comments about this book to us in care of zreview@zondervan.com. Thank you.

ZONDERVAN

Seven Days That Divide the World
Copyright © 2011 by John C. Lennox

This title is also available as a Zondervan ebook.
Visit www.zondervan.com/ebooks.

This title is also available in a Zondervan audio edition.
Visit www.zondervan.fm.

Requests for information should be addressed to:

Zondervan, *Grand Rapids, Michigan 49530*

ISBN 978-0-310-49460-7

International Trade Paper Edition

Cover design: Rob Monacelli
Interior design: Ben Fetterley & Matthew VanZomeren

Printed in the United States of America

12 13 14 15 16 /DCI/ 19 18 17 16 15 14 13 12 11 10 9 8 7 6 5 4

For Larry Taunton, whose idea it was

CONTENTS

INTRODUCTION

BEGINNING AT THE BEGINNING

"In the beginning, God created the heavens and the earth." These majestic words introduce the most translated, most printed, and most read book in history. I well remember how profoundly they affected me on Christmas Eve 1968, when, as a student at Cambridge University, I heard them read to the watching world on live television by the crew of Apollo 8 as they orbited the moon. The context was a triumphant achievement of science and technology that caught the imagination of the millions of people who watched it. To celebrate that success the astronauts chose to read a text that needed no added explanation or qualification, even though it was written millennia ago. The biblical announcement of the fact of creation was as timelessly clear as it was magnificently appropriate.

However, as distinct from the fact of creation, when it comes to the timing and means of creation, particularly the interpretation of the famous sequence of days with which the book begins, people over the centuries have found the book of Genesis less easy to understand. Indeed, controversy about this matter is at an all-time high, with the debate about teaching creationism and evolution in schools in the USA, the question of faith schools in the UK,[1] and, perhaps most of all, the popular perception of Christianity as unscientific (or even antiscientific) because of the Genesis account—a perception that is vocally endorsed by the New Atheists.

I once met a brilliant professor of literature from a famous university in a country where it was not easy to discuss the Bible publicly. She was intrigued to learn that I was a scientist who believed the Bible, and she said that she would like to ask me a question she had always wanted to ask but never dared to. She also said, with typically Eastern sensitivity, that she was reluctant to ask me the question in case it offended me: "We were taught at school that the Bible starts with a very silly, unscientific story of how the world was made in seven days. What do you have to say about it as a scientist?"

This book is written for people like her, who have been putting off even considering the Christian faith for this kind of reason. It is also written for the many convinced Christians who are disturbed not only by the controversy but also by the fact that even those who take the Bible seriously do not agree on the interpretation of the creation account. Some think that the only faithful interpretation of Scripture is the young-earth, literal view of the Genesis days that was made famous by Archbishop Ussher (1581 – 1656) of the city of Armagh in Northern Ireland—where, incidentally, I lived for the first eighteen years of my life. Ussher gave 4004 BC as the date for the origin of the earth. His calculation, based on taking the days of Genesis 1 as twenty-four-hour days of one earth week at the beginning of the universe, is six orders of magnitude away from the current scientific estimate of around four billion years.

Others hold that the text can be understood in concord with contemporary science. Such old-earth creationists are again split over the validity of Darwin's theory of evolution valid, others not. Finally, yet others argue that the Genesis account is written to communicate timeless theological truth and that attempts to harmonise it with science are misguided.

The topic is clearly a potential minefield. Yet I do not think that the situation is hopeless. For a start, there are many Christians who, like me, are convinced of the inspiration and authority of Scripture and have spent their lives actively engaged in science. We think that, since God is the author both of his Word the Bible and of the universe, there must ultimately be harmony between correct interpretation of the biblical data and correct interpretation of the scientific data. Indeed, it was the conviction that there was a creative intelligence behind the universe and the laws of nature that gave the prime stimulus and momentum to the modern scientific quest to understand nature and its laws in the sixteenth and seventeenth centuries. Furthermore, science—far from making God redundant and irrelevant, as atheists often affirm—actually confirms his existence, which is the theme of my book *God's Undertaker: Has Science Buried God?*[2]

ORGANISATION OF THE BOOK

This book has five chapters and five appendices. As an introduction to controversy and how we handle it, the first chapter discusses the challenge which the scientific theory that the earth was moving in space posed to generally accepted biblical interpretation in the sixteenth-century. The second chapter moves on to some principles of biblical interpretation and applies them to that controversy. The third is the heart of the book, where we consider the interpretation of the Genesis days. The fourth is given over to the biblical account of the origin of human beings, their antiquity, and related theological questions about death. Finally, in the fifth chapter we balance our discussion of the creation week by drawing on the New Testament in order to learn what aspects of the Genesis 1 creation narrative are emphasized there, and why they are relevant for us today.

The appendices deal with several issues that, though important, are placed at the end of the book so that the reader can engage with the main biblical material without many digressions. Appendix A looks at the background of Genesis, in terms of culture and literature. Appendix B is devoted to what is called the cosmic temple view of Genesis 1. Appendix C describes the convergence of Genesis and science over the fact that space-time had a beginning. Appendix D considers the question of whether there is conflict between Genesis 1 and Genesis 2. Finally, appendix E considers theistic evolution, with special attention paid to the so-called God-of-the-gaps arguments.

I would like to emphasise that this little book does not pretend to be exhaustive in its scope. It has been written in response to frequent requests over the years. In order to keep the book short, I have had to prioritise those issues about which I have been most often questioned. Many other interesting questions have had to be omitted.

NOTES

1. These are confessional schools of Jewish, Christian, Muslim, or any other religious foundation.
2. John C. Lennox, *God's Undertaker: Has Science Buried God?* (Oxford: Lion Hudson, 2009).

CHAPTER ONE

BUT DOES IT MOVE? A LESSON FROM HISTORY

THIS BOOK IS ABOUT a very controversial topic. Disagreement about it has been rather acrimonious at times. However, even though I am Irish, I am not going to suggest that the best way to approach it is to have a good fight! Indeed, in order to get some kind of perspective on the way we handle controversy, I wish to go back to another major controversy, one that arose in the sixteenth century. If I had been writing a book at that time, I might well have been addressing the question, what are we to think of astronomer Nicholas Copernicus's suggestion that the earth moves, when Scripture seems to teach that the earth is immovably fixed in space?

This may not seem to be a huge deal nowadays, but at the time it was a very hot topic. The reason? In the fourth century BC the famous Greek philosopher Aristotle taught that the earth was fixed in the centre of the universe and that the sun, stars, and planets revolved around it.[1] This fixed-earth view held sway for centuries even though, as early as 250 BC, Aristarchus of Samos proposed a heliocentric[2] system. After all, it made a lot of sense to ordinary people: the sun appears to go round the earth; and, if the earth moves, why aren't we all flung off into space? Why does a stone, thrown straight up into the air, come straight down if the earth is rotating rapidly? Why don't we feel a strong wind blowing in our faces in the opposite direction to our motion? Surely the idea that the earth moves is absurd?

Aristotle's work was translated into Latin, and in the Middle Ages, with the aid of the massive intellect of Thomas Aquinas (1225 – 1274), it came to influence the Roman Catholic Church.

We note in passing that Aristotle believed not only that the universe was old, but that it had always existed. Aquinas had no difficulty reconciling an eternal universe with the existence of God as Creator in a philosophical sense, but he admitted that there was difficulty reconciling it with the Bible, since the Bible clearly said there had been a beginning. The fixed earth was different: it seemed to fit in well with what the Bible said. For instance:

> Tremble before him, all the earth; yes, the world is established; it shall never be moved. (1 Chron. 16:30)

> Yes, the world is established; it shall never be moved. (Ps. 93:1)

> He set the earth on its foundations, so that it should never be moved. (Ps. 104:5)

> For the pillars of the earth are the LORD's, and on them he
> has set the world. (1 Sam. 2:8)

Furthermore, the Bible seemed not only to teach that the earth was fixed; it seemed equally clearly to say that the sun moved:

> In them he has set a tent for the sun, which comes out like
> a bridegroom leaving his chamber, and, like a strong man,
> runs its course with joy. Its rising is from the end of the heav-
> ens, and its circuit to the end of them, and there is nothing
> hidden from its heat. (Ps. 19:4–6)

> The sun rises, and the sun goes down, and hastens to the
> place where it rises. (Eccl. 1:5)

So it is not surprising that when in 1543 Copernicus published his famous work *On the Revolutions of the Celestial Orbs,* in which he advanced the view that the earth and the planets orbited the sun, this startling new scientific theory was called into question by Protestants and Catholics alike. It is alleged that even before Copernicus published his book, Martin Luther had rejected the heliocentric point of view in rather strong terms in his *Table Talk* (1539):

> There is talk of a new astrologer who wants to prove that the
> earth moves and goes around instead of the sky, the sun, the
> moon, just as if somebody were moving in a carriage or ship
> might hold that he was sitting still and at rest while the earth
> and the trees walked and moved. But that is how things are
> nowadays: when a man wishes to be clever he must ... invent
> something special, and the way he does it must needs be
> the best! The fool wants to turn the whole art of astronomy
> upside-down. However, as Holy Scripture tells us, so did
> Joshua bid the sun to stand still and not the earth.[3]

Many of Luther's comments in *Table Talk* were made tongue in cheek, and there is considerable debate about the authenticity of this quote. Historian John Hedley Brooke writes, "Whether Luther really referred to Copernicus as a fool has been doubted, but in an off-the-cuff dismissal he remembered that Joshua had told the sun, not the earth, to stand still."[4]

John Calvin, on the other hand, clearly believed that the earth was fixed: "By what means could it [the earth] maintain itself unmoved, while the heavens above are in constant rapid motion, did not its Divine Maker fix and establish it?"[5]

Some years after Copernicus, in 1632, Galileo challenged the Aristotelian view in his famous book *Dialogue concerning the Two Chief World Systems.* This incident has gone down in history as an iconic example of how religion is antagonistic to science. Yet Galileo, far from being an atheist, was driven by his deep inner conviction that the Creator, who had "endowed us with senses, reason and intellect," intended us not to "forgo their use and by some other means to give us knowledge which we can attain by them."[6] Galileo held that the laws of nature are written by the hand of God in the "language of mathematics"[7] and that the "human mind is a work of God and one of the most excellent."[8]

Galileo was attacked for his theory of a moving earth, first by the Aristotelian philosophers, and then by the Roman Catholic Church. The issue at stake was clear: Galileo's science was threatening the all-pervasive Aristotelianism of both academy and church. The conflict was far more between two "scientific" world-pictures than between science and religion. In the end, Galileo had to "recant" under pressure but still (according to the story) could not help muttering to his inquisitors, "But it does move."

There is, of course, no excuse whatsoever for the Roman Catholic Church's use of the Inquisition to muzzle Galileo, nor for its subsequently taking several centuries to rehabilitate him. Yet, again contrary to popular belief, Galileo was never tortured, and his subsequent house arrest was spent, for the most part, in luxurious private residences belonging to friends. Furthermore, the scientist brought some of his problems on himself by his lack of tact.

Many historians of science conclude that the Galileo affair really does nothing to confirm the simplistic conflict view of the relationship of science to religion.[9]

It subsequently took many years to establish the heliocentric view, which my readers, I presume, now accept, being quite comfortable with the idea that not only does the earth rotate about its own axis, but it moves in an elliptical orbit round the sun at an average of 30 km/sec (about 67,000 mph), taking a year to complete the circuit.

But now we need to face an important question: why do Christians accept this "new" interpretation, and not still insist on a "literal" understanding of the "pillars of the earth"? Why are we not still split up into fixed-earthers and moving-earthers? Is it really because we have all compromised, and made Scripture subservient to science?

NOTES

1. Often referred to as the Ptolemaic system.
2. *Heliocentric* means "with the sun at the centre," from the Greek *helios*, "sun."

3. Martin Luther, *Table Talk*, quoted in Nicolaus Copernicus, *On the Revolutions of the Heavenly Spheres*, reprinted in *Great Books of the Western World* (Chicago: Encyclopaedia Britannica, 1939), 499–838.

4. John Hedley Brooke, *Science and Religion* (Cambridge: Cambridge University Press, 1991), 96.

5. John Calvin, *Commentary on the Book of Psalms* (Grand Rapids: Eerdmans, 1949), 4:6–7.

6. Letter to Grand Duchess Christina, 1615.

7. Stillman Drake, *Discoveries and Opinions of Galileo* (New York: Doubleday, 1957), 237.

8. Galileo Galilei, *Dialogue concerning the Two Chief World Systems*, trans. Stillman Drake (Berkeley: University of California Press, 1953), 104.

9. See John C. Lennox, *God's Undertaker: Has Science Buried God?* (Oxford: Lion Hudson, 2009), 23–26.

CHAPTER TWO

BUT DOES IT MOVE? A LESSON ABOUT SCRIPTURE

HOW SHOULD WE UNDERSTAND THE BIBLE?

The issue at stake in the Galileo controversy is, of course, how the Bible should be interpreted. So let us think about some general principles of interpretation before we apply them to the moving-earth controversy.

The first obvious, yet important thing to say about the Bible is that it is literature. In fact, it is a whole library of books: some of them history, some poetry, some in the form of letters, and so on, very different in content and style. In approaching literature in general, the first question to ask is, how does the author who wrote it wish it to be understood? For instance, the author of a mathematics textbook does not intend it to be understood as poetry; Shakespeare does not intend us to understand his plays as exact history, and so on.

Next, one should *in the first instance* be guided by the natural understanding of a passage, sentence, word, or phrase in its context, historically, culturally, and linguistically. The Reformers emphasised this in their reaction against the kind of interpretation that (to cite an ancient example) took the four rivers mentioned in Genesis 2 — the Pishon, Gihon, Tigris, and Euphrates — to represent the body, soul, spirit, and mind, respectively. By contrast with this "allegorical" method of interpretation, the Reformers adopted an approach described by the *Oxford English Dictionary* in its definition of *literal*: "that sense or interpretation (of a text) which is obtained by taking its words in their natural or customary meaning, and applying the ordinary rules of grammar; opposed to *mystical, allegorical,* etc.," and "hence, by extension, ... the primary sense of a word, or ... the sense expressed by the actual wording of a passage, as distinguished from any metaphorical or merely suggested meaning."[1] Of course, there is nothing new in this way of understanding literature: it is what all of us use every day in our reading and conversation, without even thinking about it.

The importance of considering the natural understanding of a passage is clear, when it comes to the basic teaching of the Christian faith. The crucial thing about Christianity's fundamental doctrines is that they are first and foremost to be understood in their natural, primary sense. The cross of Christ is not primarily a metaphor. It involved an actual death. The resurrection is not primarily an allegory. It was a physical event: a "standing up again"[2] of a body that had died.

But this basic principle needs to be qualified. For instance, when we are dealing with a text that was produced in a culture distant from our own both in time and in geography, what we think the natural meaning is may not have been the natural meaning for those to whom the text was originally addressed. We shall consider this issue in due course.

At this stage we make a few general remarks about the way in which we use language. Some of us will be familiar with what I am about to say, but many of us may not have thought much about *how* we use language—we are too busy using it to bother. However, it will help us greatly if we spend just a little time thinking about this matter.

Firstly, there can be more than one natural reading of a word or phrase. For example, in Genesis 1 there are several instances of this. The word "earth" is first used for the planet, and then a little later for the dry land as distinct from the sea. Both times the word *earth* is clearly meant literally, but the two meanings are different, as is clear from their context.

Next, in many places a literal understanding will not work. Let's take first an example from everyday speech. We all understand what a person means when they say, "The car was flying down the road." The car and the road are very literal, but "flying" is a metaphor. However, we also are well aware that the metaphor "flying" stands for something very real that could be expressed more literally as "driving fast." Just because a sentence contains a metaphor, it doesn't mean that it is not referring to something real.

For a biblical example, take Jesus' statement, "I am the door" (John 10:9). It is clearly not meant to be understood in the primary, literal sense of a door made of wood. It is meant metaphorically. But notice again that the metaphor stands for something real: Jesus is a real doorway into an actual, and therefore very literal, experience of salvation and eternal life. We should also note that the reason why we do not take this statement literally has to do with our experience of the world. We know about doors, and our experience of them helps us decide that Jesus is using a metaphor. We shall return to this point later.

Furthermore, it is impossible, as C. S. Lewis pointed out, to speak of things beyond our immediate senses without using metaphor. Scientists, therefore, use metaphor all the time. They talk about light particles and wave packets of energy; but they don't intend you to imagine light as literal tiny balls, or energy as literal waves on the sea. Yet in each case the metaphor is describing something real — literal, if you like — at a higher level.

To make things more complicated, but also more interesting, sometimes both a primary and a metaphorical sense can occur together. Take the ascension of Christ, for example. In its primary sense it refers to the literal, vertical ascent of Jesus into the sky that was physically observed by the disciples.[3] However, there is more to it than that. The literal upward movement carries a deeper meaning — he ascended to the throne of God. For instance, when we say that Queen Elizabeth II ascended the throne of England in 1952, we do not simply mean that she got up onto an ornate chair in Westminster Abbey. She did that, of course; but that (literal) getting up on the chair was at the same time a metaphor for her (literal) assumption of real power over her people. Similarly, the (literal) ascension of Christ is a metaphor of his (literal) assumption of universal authority.

In each of these examples we see how the word *literal* can turn out to be inadequate and even misleading, since there can be different levels of literality. It is therefore common nowadays to reserve the word *literalistic* for an adherence to the basic, primary meaning of a word or expression, and *literal* for the natural reading as intended by the author or speaker. Thus, reading the phrase "the car was flying down the road" in a literalistic way would mean understanding the car to be actually flying. Reading it literally—that is, in the natural sense—would mean that the car was going very fast. However, this usage of *literal* is not agreed by all, which often leads to confusion. We must, therefore, be careful with our use of *literal*.

I recall once talking about the Genesis creation narrative with a well-known astrophysicist, who suggested to me that it was primitive to believe the Bible. To illustrate a point, I wrote on his blackboard: "And God said, let there be light. And there was light." He said: "That sounds really primitive. You don't really believe it, do you? It suggests that God has a physical voice box and speaks like we do." In other words, my colleague was taking the word "said" in its primary, natural, human sense—he was taking it literalistically. I laughed, and told him that it was now he who was being primitive. Of course God, who is spirit, doesn't have a physical voice box, but he can communicate. In other words, the expression "And God said" denotes real, literal communication, but we do not have the slightest idea as to how it is done.

The word *said* means something different for God than it does for us,[4] but the two usages are sufficiently related for one word to do both jobs effectively. The reason I was amused when my astrophysicist friend made his remarks is that, as I reminded him, scientists use metaphors all the time without batting an eyelid. They, of all people, should not complain when the Bible uses them.

As a general point, it is worth recalling a perceptive remark made by Henri Blocher: "Human speech rarely remains at the zero-point of plain prose, which communicates in the simplest and most direct manner, using words in their ordinary sense."[5] What Blocher means is that we all use metaphors in our ordinary conversation. How colourless life would be without them.

There is more that could be said about the use of language, but perhaps we now have enough to grasp the basic idea. And I am sure the last thing the reader wants is for this book to turn into a lengthy lesson in English grammar!

It would be a pity if, in a desire (rightly) to treat the Bible as more than a book, we ended up treating it as less than a book by not permitting it the range and use of language, order, and figures of speech that are (or ought to be) familiar to us from our ordinary experience of conversation and reading.

If we take this into account, the answer to the question, at what level should a text be read? is often obvious. We take the natural, primary meaning; and if that doesn't make sense, we go for the next level. For example, Jesus' statements "I am the door" (John 10:9) and "I am the bread of life" (John 6:48). But there are instances where the answer does not seem to be so obvious, in the sense that believers in all ages who are fully convinced of the authority of Scripture come to different interpretations. What should we do in such a situation? That was the hot-button question in the time of Galileo. Let us therefore now apply what we have learned to the moving-earth controversy, to see how

Christians eventually came to accept this "new" interpretation and ceased to insist on a literalistic understanding of the foundations and pillars of the earth.

Of course, this did not happen overnight. For many years, if not centuries, there would have been two major polarised positions: the fixed-earthers and the moving-earthers — with the latter group growing in number all the time. These positions were held, not only by people for whom Scripture had little or no authority (although there must have been some such), but by those who were convinced that the Bible was the inspired Word of God and who regarded it as the full and final authority. The latter would agree on the core elements of the gospel, including the doctrines of creation; the fall; salvation; the incarnation, life, death, burial, resurrection, and ascension of Christ; the expectation of his return; and the final judgement. They disagreed, however, on what Scripture taught about the motion of the earth.

This immediately raises several questions. Were these differences simply driven by a desire on the part of the moving-earth faction to fit in with advances in science; or were they the result of intransigence and antiscientific attitudes on the part of the fixed-earth faction? Did the moving-earthers necessarily compromise the integrity and authority of Scripture?

THE BIBLE AND SCIENCE

First, some general comments. It is often said that the Bible is not relevant to science at all. Indeed, well-known American palaeontologist Stephen Jay Gould of Harvard University suggested that religion and science belong to separate domains or magisteria.[6] He meant that science and religion deal with fundamentally distinct questions, and harmony can be achieved if we keep the two completely apart.

Now this view (often referred to by the acronym NOMA—nonoverlapping magisteria) has an obvious attraction for some people: if science and the Bible have nothing to do with each other, then our problem is solved. However, there are two very big snags. Firstly, the claim that science and religion are completely separate often conceals another belief: that science deals with reality, and religion with Santa Claus, the Tooth Fairy, and God. The impression that science deals with truth and religion deals with fantasy is very widespread. No one who is convinced of the truth, inspiration, and authority of Scripture could agree with that.

But there is another snag with Gould's view. We cannot keep science and Scripture completely separate, for the simple reason that the Bible talks about some of the things that science talks about. And they are very important things—like the origin of the universe and of life. They are also foundational both to science and to philosophy. "In the beginning, God created the heavens and the earth" (Gen. 1:1) and "God created man in his own image" (Gen. 1:27) are statements about the objective physical universe and the status of human beings, with very far-reaching implications for our understanding of the universe and of ourselves.

Let me make my position clear. I am a scientist who believes Scripture to be the Word of God. I am not shy, therefore, of drawing scientific implications from it, where warranted. However, saying Scripture has scientific implications does not mean that the Bible is a scientific treatise from which we can deduce Newton's Laws, Einstein's equations, or the chemical structure of common salt. John Calvin wrote in his commentary on Genesis, "Nothing is here treated of but the visible form of the world. He who would learn astronomy, and other recondite arts, let him go elsewhere."[7]

Indeed, one of the fascinating tasks we are encouraged to do in God's universe is to do just that—to find out many things for ourselves. Remember, according to Genesis, it was God himself who told the first humans to name the animals: he was not going to do it for them (Gen. 2:19–20). That is very interesting, because naming things is the very essence of science (we call it taxonomy); and so it was God who started science off! It was for this kind of reason that the brilliant scientist James Clerk-Maxwell had the words of Psalm 111:2 (KJV) engraved on the Cavendish Laboratory in Cambridge: "The works of the LORD are great, sought out of all them that have pleasure therein." God loves an enquiring mind, a fact that has been a great encouragement to me in my study of mathematics and the history and philosophy of science.

We can surely also agree that the Bible is not written in advanced contemporary scientific language. This circumstance should not cause us any surprise or difficulty, but rather gratitude and relief. Suppose, for instance, that God had intended to explain the origin of the universe and life to us in detailed scientific language. Science is constantly changing, developing, standing in need of correction, although (we trust) becoming more and more accurate. If the biblical explanation were at the level, say, of twenty-second-century science, it would likely be unintelligible to everyone, including scientists today. This could scarcely have been God's intention. He wished his meaning to be accessible to all.[8] Indeed, one of the most remarkable things about Genesis is that it is accessible to, and has a message for, everyone, whether or not they are scientifically literate. As John Calvin put it, "The Holy Spirit had no intention to teach astronomy; and, in proposing instruction meant to be common to the simplest and most uneducated persons, he made use by Moses and the other prophets of popular language ... The Holy Spirit would rather speak childishly than unintelligibly to the humble and unlearned."[9] This statement, be it noted, does not come from someone who was vague about the authority of Scripture; nor is it a recent reflection produced by the alleged embarrassment of Christians confronted by modern science. Indeed, Augustine (354–430) had already had the same thought a thousand years before Calvin: "We do not read in the Gospel that the Lord said that I send to you the Paraclete who will teach you about the course of the sun and the moon, for he wanted to make Christians and not mathematicians."

Rather than scientific language, the Bible often uses what is called phenomenological language—the language of appearance. It describes what anyone can see. It talks about the sun rising just as everyone else does, including scientists, even though they know that the sun only appears to rise because of the rotation of the earth. Saying that the sun "rises" does not commit the Bible, or a scientist for that matter, to any particular model of the solar system.

Having said all that, however, let us once again emphasise the key issue. The Bible, though not a textbook of science, precisely because it is God's revealed Word, has *truth* to tell us about the same kind of objective reality that science discusses, in particular about the nature and origin of the cosmos and of human beings. We must therefore try to understand that truth.

In *On the Literal Meaning of Genesis*, Augustine offered Christians some interesting and valuable advice on how to engage with science. His advice shows that our scientifically advanced era is not the only one to be aware of the kind of tension precipitated by a perceived conflict between science and the biblical record. Augustine was well acquainted with it in his own day.[10] What he has to say is worth quoting at some length in order to capture its spirit:

> Usually, even a non-Christian knows something about the earth, the heavens ... and this knowledge he holds to as being certain from reason and experience. Now, it is a disgraceful and dangerous thing for an infidel to hear a Christian, presumably giving the meaning of Holy Scripture, talking nonsense on these topics; and we should take all means to prevent such an embarrassing situation, in which people show up vast ignorance in a Christian and laugh it to scorn ... If they find a Christian mistaken in a field which they themselves know well and hear him maintaining his foolish opinions about our books, how are they going to believe those books in matters concerning the resurrection of the dead, the hope of eternal life, and the kingdom of heaven, when they think their pages are full of falsehoods and on facts which they themselves have learnt from experience and the light of reason?[11]

Augustine has surely put his finger on one of the reasons none of us would maintain a base-level literalistic interpretation of the foundations and pillars of the earth: we don't wish to appear scientifically illiterate[12] and bring the Christian message into disrepute. Of course (but it needs to be said) Augustine is not suggesting that Christians should not be prepared to face ridicule over fundamental doctrines of the Christian message, like the deity of Christ, his resurrection, and so on. Such ridicule, often based on the false notion that science has made it impossible to believe in miracles,[13] has been evident from the very beginnings of Christianity and still occurs today, as the present author has cause to know. The take-home message from Augustine is, rather, that, if my views on something not fundamental to the gospel, on which equally convinced Christians disagree, attract ridicule and therefore disincline my hearers to listen to anything I have to say about the Christian message, then I should be prepared to entertain the possibility that it might be my interpretation that is at fault.

Most of us would surely agree that it is important to distinguish between matters that belong to the core message of the Bible and issues that are less central, where there is room for variation in opinion.[14] We also need to be prepared to distinguish between what Scripture actually says and what we think it means. It is Scripture that has the final authority, not our understanding of it. It is a sad spectacle, and one that brings discredit on the Christian message, when those who profess to believe that message belie their profession by fighting among themselves or caricaturing others, rather than engaging in respectful discussion through which all sides might just learn something.

In connection with the motion of the earth, we accept Augustine's advice because we can now see that, although the Bible texts *could* be understood to support a fixed earth, there is a *reasonable* alternative interpretation of those texts that makes far more sense in light of our greater understanding of how the solar system operates.

We know now that the earth does not rest on literal foundations or pillars made of stone, concrete, or steel. We can therefore see that the words "foundations" and "pillars" are used in a metaphorical sense. However, it needs to be emphasised once more that the metaphors stand for realities. God the Creator has built certain very real stabilities into the planetary system that will guarantee its existence so long as is necessary to fulfil his purposes. Science has been able to show us that the earth is stable in its orbit over long periods of time, thanks in part to the obedience of gravity to an inverse square law, to the presence of the moon, which stabilises the tilt of earth's axis, and to the existence of the giant planet Jupiter, which helps keep the other planets in the same orbital plane.[15] Earth's stability, therefore, is very real. It is, if you wish, a literal or true stability, even though it does not now make sense to understand the word *stability* literalistically, as referring to motionlessness.

But there is something more. We accept the metaphorical interpretation because we can see that it is a perfectly sensible and informed understanding of the biblical text. The earth does not have to be at the centre of the physical universe in order to be a centre of God's attention. Even though our interpretation relies on scientific knowledge, it does not compromise the authority of Scripture. And this is the important point. Scripture has the primary authority. Experience and science have helped decide between the possible interpretations that Scripture allows.

The vast majority of Christians are therefore perfectly happy with a metaphorical interpretation of the foundations and pillars of the earth. They do not regard it as contrived or subservient to science, even though science has helped them refine and adjust their interpretation.

What, then, should we think of the believers of earlier generations who, for hundreds of years, interpreted the biblical record in terms of a fixed earth? Would we accuse them of not believing the gospel and Scripture, just because they did not know what we now know? Of course not. For them that interpretation made sense of Scripture and fitted in with the best science of the day. Indeed, no one in the ancient world had evidence that the earth moved (although some, like Aristarchus of Samos, had guessed it).

Regarding the attitude of Luther and Calvin, John Hedley Brooke is insightful: "The important point is not whether Luther and Calvin happened to make peremptory remarks, exuding a lifetime's confidence in a pre-Copernican cosmology, but whether their exegetical principles implied an inevitable clash as the new system gained in plausibility."[16] And Brooke suggests they did not.

Interestingly, the first hard evidence that the earth moved was not found until 1725, when James Bradley, Savilian Professor of Astronomy at Oxford and later Astronomer Royal, deduced it from his observation of the aberration of the star Gamma Draconis.[17] The earlier Christian interpretation of Scripture in terms of a fixed earth did not attract the ridicule of nonbelievers, since fixed earth was the dominant view in society as a whole at the time. For many centuries most people never even bothered to question it, simply because there was no reason to do so.

However, once it became generally evident and accepted that the earth did move, and that the Scriptures could be interpreted consistently with that fact without compromising their integrity or authority, thereafter to maintain that Scripture insisted that the earth was fixed in the sky would leave one open to justifiable ridicule, and would bring Scripture into disrepute.

FINAL LESSONS FROM GALILEO

The Galileo incident teaches us that we should be humble enough to distinguish between what the Bible says and our interpretations of it. The biblical text might just be more sophisticated than we first imagined, and we might therefore be in danger of using it to support ideas that it never intended to teach. The Bible could be understood to teach that the earth was fixed. But it does not have to be understood that way. At least, Galileo thought so in his day, and history has subsequently proved him right.

Another lesson in a different direction, but one not often drawn, is that it was Galileo (who believed in the Bible) who was advancing a better *scientific* understanding of the universe. He was doing so, as we have seen, not only against the obscurantism of some churchmen, but (and first of all) against the resistance (and obscurantism) of the secular philosophers of his time, who, like the churchmen, were convinced disciples of Aristotle. Philosophers and scientists today also have need of humility in light of facts, even if those facts are being pointed out by a believer in God! Lack of belief in God is no more a guarantee of scientific orthodoxy than is belief in God. What is clear, concerning both Galileo's time and ours, is that criticism of a reigning scientific paradigm[18] is fraught with risk, no matter who engages in it.

Finally we see that there are two extremes to be avoided. The first is the danger of tying interpretation of Scripture too closely to the science of the day, as the fixed-earthers did—even though, as we have seen, it is hard to blame them in light of the fact that this view was then the reigning *scientific* paradigm. Indeed, it is for this reason that I prefer to speak of the *convergence* between interpretations of Scripture and science at a particular time—for example, the current convergence that there was a beginning, which we shall consider in due course.

The opposite danger is to ignore science. This, as Augustine warned, brings the gospel into disrepute. It is also an obscurantist attitude that finds no support in Scripture. In Romans 1:20, Paul, speaking about God, writes, "For his invisible attributes, namely, his eternal power and divine nature, have been clearly perceived, ever since the creation of the world, in the things that have been made. So they are without excuse." If, therefore, we can learn things about God as Creator from the visible universe, it is surely incumbent upon us to use our God-given minds to think about what these things are, and thus to relate God's general revelation in nature to his special revelation in his Word so that we can rejoice in both. After all, it was God who put the universe there, and it would be very strange if we had no interest in it.

Finding a balance is not always easy—but we seem to have managed it over the issue of the motion of the earth, even though it only took about seventeen hundred years to get there! I sincerely hope that this means there is hope for us on other controversies. We are about to consider one right now.

NOTES

1. This is often called "the literal method." We shall discuss the use of the word *literal* below.

2. This is the meaning of the Greek word *anastasis*, used in the New Testament for "resurrection."

3. See Acts 1, written, it should be observed, by the historian Luke, who, as a doctor, had the nearest approximation to a scientific education of any of the New Testament writers. For Luke's appreciation of the questions arising in connection with science and miracle, see David W. Gooding, *According to Luke* (Leicester, UK: Inter-Varsity, 1987), 37ff. For a scientific viewpoint see John C. Lennox, *God's Undertaker: Has Science Buried God?* (Oxford: Lion Hudson, 2009), chap. 12.

4. Indeed, when God speaks to certain people in the Bible, he uses human language, though how he does so is, of course, unknown to us. One might go further and say that God's speech is the primary kind and that human speech is derivative—in the sense that we are made in God's image.

5. Henri Blocher, *In the Beginning* (Leicester, UK: Inter-Varsity, 1984), 18.

6. A magisterium is a body of teaching.

7. John Calvin, *Commentaries on the First Book of Moses, Called Genesis*, trans. John King (Grand Rapids: Eerdmans, 1988), 1:79.

8. We might also note that biblical Hebrew has a vocabulary of fewer than four thousand words, whereas in English roughly two hundred thousand words are in current use.

9. John Calvin, *Commentary on the Book of Psalms,* vol. V (Edinburgh: T. Constable, 1849), v. 7, p. 184.

10. Please note that I don't mean a twenty-four-hour day here—but more of that later!

11. Augustine, *The Literal Meaning of Genesis,* vol. 1 (Mahwah, NJ: Paulist Press, 1982), chap. 19, v. 39, p. 42.

12. Although I note that there still exists today a website maintaining the Aristotelian view: www.fixedearth.com.

13. See Lennox, *God's Undertaker*, chap. 12.

14. Of course there will often be difference of opinion as to what is central and what is peripheral.

15. From a mathematical point of view there are some chaotic elements in the dynamics of the planets. We cannot predict accurately where they will be situated in 100 million years' time, because we cannot measure them accurately enough now. However, these chaotic elements appear to be bounded.

16. John Hedley Brooke, *Science and Religion* (Cambridge: Cambridge University Press, 1991), 96.

17. A star that passes directly overhead in London. Bradley detected an annual variation in the apparent position of stars that was due to changes in the earth's velocity. Such calculations lead to an estimate for earth's orbital velocity of 30 km/sec.

18. A paradigm is a big picture or framework within which science is done.

CHAPTER THREE

BUT IS IT OLD? THE DAYS OF CREATION

INTERPRETATION OF THE GENESIS DAYS: A BRIEF HISTORICAL PERSPECTIVE

We all know what the controversy is. Christians are divided into two main groups in their understanding of the Genesis days. First, there are those who believe that the days of Genesis are the twenty-four-hour days of one earth week, and that the universe is young (created around six thousand years ago). Then there are those who believe that the universe is ancient. It is important to take on board right away that both the young-earth and the ancient-earth creationist views go back a long way. Neither of them is a recent invention.

The word *creationist*, however, has changed its meaning over time. Originally it meant simply someone who believed in a creator, without any implication for how or when the creating was done; nowadays, *creationist* is usually taken to mean "young-earth creationist."

Through the ages many have held that straight lines can be drawn from the creation week of Genesis to the week of ordinary life. The Jewish calendar, for instance, has for centuries taken as its starting point the "Era of Creation," which it dates to 3761 BC (2010 is the Jewish year 5770—which runs from September 2009 to September 2010). Furthermore, in contemporary Hebrew, the days of the week are denoted by the numbers 1–6, with the seventh day Shabbat (Sabbath, rest), exactly as in Genesis 1.

The Christian reformers Luther and Calvin[1] and many of those who drew up the Westminster Confession also held the twenty-four-hour view. In his commentary on Genesis, Calvin said that the duration of creation was "the space of six days," a phrase later adopted into the Westminster Confession.

However, there have been others, even in ancient times, who interpreted Genesis 1 differently. Among them was Philo (10 BC–AD 50), an influential Jewish writer who lived in Alexandria at the time of Christ. Among many other works, he wrote a book entitled *A Treatise on the Account of the Creation of the World as Given by Moses*. In section III.13 he says that "the world was made in six days, not because the Creator stood in need of a length of time (for it is natural that God should do everything at once, not merely by uttering a command, but by even thinking of it); but because the things created required arrangement; and number is akin to arrangement; and, of all numbers, six is, by the laws of nature, the most productive: for of all the numbers, from the unit upwards, it is the first perfect one, being made equal to its parts, and being made complete by them; the number three being half of it, and the number two a third of it, and the unit a sixth of it ..." Thus Philo thought creation was the act of a moment, and the Genesis record had more to do with principles of order and arrangement.

Some of the early church fathers, such as Justin Martyr, in his *Dialogue with Trypho*, and Irenaeus, in *Against Heresies*, suggested that the days might have been long epochs, on the basis of Psalm 90:4 ("For a thousand years in your sight are but as yesterday when it is past, or as a watch in the night") and 2 Peter 3:8 ("With the Lord one day is as a thousand years, and a thousand years as one day"). Irenaeus applied this reading of Genesis to the warning God gave regarding the Tree of the Knowledge of Good and Evil ("In the day that you eat of it you shall surely die" [Gen. 2:17]): "On one and the same day on which they ate, they also died (for it is one day of creation) ... He (Adam) did not overstep the thousand years, but died within their limit."[2]

Clement of Alexandria (AD 150–215), writing, like Justin and Irenaeus, in the second century, thought that creation could not take place in time at all, since "time was born along with things which exist."[3] He therefore understood the days to communicate the priority of created things but not the timing of their creation. A little later, Origen (AD 185–254), the most prominent theologian of his time, pointed out that in the Genesis account the sun was not made until the fourth day. He made the obvious objection: "Now what man of intelligence will believe that the first, the second and the third day, and the evening and morning existed without the sun, moon and stars?"[4] We shall consider his objection in the next chapter.

In the fourth century, Augustine, who wrote much about Genesis, openly stated in his book *The City of God* that he found the days of Genesis 1 difficult: "As for these days, it is difficult, perhaps impossible to think, let alone explain in words, what they mean."[5] In his famous commentary *On the Literal Meaning of Genesis*, he added: "But at least we know that it [the Genesis day] is different from the ordinary day with which we are familiar." In fact Augustine (like Philo above) held that God had created everything in a moment, and that the days represented a logical sequence to explain it to us.

These men were not armchair theorists. Some of them were tortured or martyred for their faith: among them Justin Martyr (as his name implies), Irenaeus, and Origen. Nor, obviously, were they influenced by contemporary science, such as geology and evolutionary biology.

We have only given some examples in this very brief survey; hence it is important to add that the understanding of the days of Genesis as twenty-four-hour days seems to have been the dominant view for many centuries.

One of the major tensions in the discussion of the early chapters of Genesis is between those who think that the author intended the book to be read as history and those who regard the author's intention as the conveying of timeless truths through figurative, theological language.

I say "the early chapters," since the impression given by the rest of the book of Genesis is that of a historical narrative which describes the rise of the Hebrew nation from among the Gentile nations of the ancient Near East, and follows their chronological development through the family histories of Abraham, Isaac, and Jacob. It is not surprising, then, that many argue the same for the early chapters of Genesis, which clearly form an integral part of the book. Surely those chapters also give a strong impression that they are talking about actual events, places, and people, in giving a historical narrative from the creation of the world and the first humans, to the development and spread of civilization, down to the time of the great flood through which Noah and his family were preserved to become the progenitors of the nations of the ancient Near East? It seems to me that there could be a real danger in some quarters of separating theology from history.[6]

Genesis is, of course, a text that comes to us from a time and culture very different from our own. It is from the ancient Near East, so we cannot simply read it as if it were a contemporary Western document written to address contemporary Western concerns.[7]

That raises the question: just how much is Genesis influenced by the culture in which it was written, and in what sense?[8] This is a question that can be addressed to any part of the Bible, of course. Those who, like the present author, are convinced that Scripture is God's revelation are also aware that God used human authors who wrote in terms of their own culture and surroundings as they conveyed God's Word to the world. Jesus told parables about farming, building, and fishing, not about factories, aviation, and jungle exploration. And yet his parables are accessible to anyone in any age. Similarly with Genesis. Knowledge of ancient Near Eastern culture can certainly help us a great deal, but the central statements of Genesis have got that timeless quality about them that means they can be understood in 1000 BC or AD 2000.

THE MAIN VIEWS OF THE GENESIS DAYS

For some time now the two main interpretations of the days of Genesis 1 (young-earth and old-earth) have morphed into a spectrum (with many variants), running through the following main views:[9]

The 24-hour view	The days are seven 24-hour days, of one earth week, about six thousand years ago.
The day-age view	The days are in chronological order, each representing a period of time of unspecified length.
The framework view	The days exhibit a logical, rather than a chronological, order.

The meanings of views 1 and 2 are clear; but we shall briefly outline the content of view 3. The basic idea here has to do with the distinction between two kinds of order, to which we referred earlier when we noted that Clement and Augustine thought that the sequence of days in Genesis was a logical rather than a chronological sequence.

An illustration will make the difference clear. If a builder is describing how his company built a hospital, he will probably describe the process chronologically: "We dug a hole, laid foundations, and then put up the superstructure floor by floor: basement, car park; ground floor, administration; first floor, wards; second, operating theatres; third, more wards." But ask the surgeon to describe the construction of the hospital and he might say, "We put the operating theatre on the second floor and located wards above and below it on the first and third floors." The surgeon describes the hospital logically from his perspective, not chronologically. We are so used to this kind of thing that we take account of it automatically. We would not insist on understanding the surgeon as implying that the operating theatre suddenly appeared in mid-air and wards were then constructed above and below it. And yet we would know that the surgeon was describing a very real and literal hospital.

For a biblical example, compare the order given in Genesis 1 with that given in Isaiah 45:12: "I made the earth and created man on it; it was my hands that stretched out the heavens, and I commanded all their host." Would anyone think of deducing from Isaiah that God first created the earth, then humans, and finally the heavens? I think not. Isaiah's semipoetic description does not prioritise chronology. Nevertheless, I wish to stress once again that Isaiah is describing something real, events that really happened; but he is not relating them (altogether) in the order in which they happened.

The third of the major interpretations in our list, the framework view, prioritises logical order over chronological. More than two centuries ago it was suggested by Johann Gottfried von Herder (1744–1803) that the Genesis days form a literary or artistic framework.[10] In this view days 1–3 form a triad that corresponds to the triad formed by days 4–6:

Day*	Forming	Filling	Day
1	Light	Luminaries	4
2	Sky/seas	Sea creatures/ Winged creatures	5
3	Seas/dry land/ vegetation	Land animals/ humans	6

The first triad concerns giving form or structure to what was initially formless, and the second concerns filling the newly created but empty forms. Light, then, is created on day 1, and day 4 tells us about the light bearers: sun, moon, and stars. The sky and seas occur on day 2, and on day 5 the sea is filled with sea creatures and the sky with winged creatures.

It has been pointed out that the parallelism is not perfect. For instance, the light bearers of the fourth day are placed in the sky, which is first mentioned on the second day. Hence, if the first and fourth days were completely parallel, one would expect the sky to be mentioned on the first day. Also, the sea creatures of day 5 belong to the seas of day 3; or, indeed, to the deep that is mentioned right at the beginning. Nevertheless the parallelism is striking and, furthermore, is of a type found elsewhere in Scripture.[11]

A further variation of view 3 is known as "the cosmic temple view." According to John Walton, the days form a chronological sequence of twenty-four-hour days but are "not given as the period of time over which the material cosmos came into being, but the period of time devoted to the inauguration of the functions of the cosmic temple, and perhaps also its annual re-enactment."[12]

In connection with the framework view, then, the existence of parallels between the first three and the second three days does not necessarily imply that the days do not form a chronological sequence.[13] After all, at the simplest level, you cannot have plants and animals on dry land that does not yet exist. Derek Kidner's comment is apposite: "The march of the days is too majestic a progress to carry no implication of ordered sequence; it also seems over-subtle to adopt a view of the passage which discounts one of the primary impressions it makes on the ordinary reader."[14]

Quite so. Indeed, the fact that the days are given an explicit numerical sequence, together with the grammatical observation that the verbal forms used in the narrative are those whose "ordinary usage in narrative is to denote discrete and basically sequential events,"[15] makes a strong case that ordered *chronological* sequence is intended. The existence of the framework might then indicate that there is *more* to the text than ordered sequence: sequence and framework are not necessarily mutually exclusive.

What then should we think of the different interpretations? Well, the first thing we should note is that they are *different* interpretations of the same *text*. That much is obvious. But it has a very important implication, which is that we shall need to think hard about *what the text says* before trying to decide which interpretation makes most sense of it.

Now this is sometimes easier said than done, since all of us bring preconceived ideas to the understanding of any text. Yet experience shows that problems in interpreting a passage often spring from failing to see exactly what the text says because we are impatient to get at the meaning. Of course, in practice it is sometimes difficult to disentangle what we think the text says from what we think it means; but it is nevertheless worth holding the distinction in mind as we proceed. If we believe in the inspiration of Scripture, we must take the text seriously because it is Scripture that is inspired and not my particular understanding of it, as I said earlier. One way of doing this is to try to read Genesis 1 as if we had never read it before.

Let's now look at a table of contents of the first section of Genesis, 1:1–2:3:

1. Statement regarding the creation of the heavens and the earth: 1:1–2
2. Six days of God's creation and organisational activity, culminating in the creation of human beings in his image: 1:3—2:1
3. The seventh day, day of God's rest—Sabbath: 2:2–3

The initial, unmistakeable impression is that of a chronological sequence of events, giving the briefest of brief histories of time. The narrative starts with a world "without form and void" (1:2). It then describes how God speaks and through his creative Word, day by day, step by step, shapes and fills the world, so that it is finally fit for habitation by creatures that uniquely bear God's image and likeness— human beings. This movement towards a goal accords with the later statement in Isaiah to the effect that God did not create the world empty but created it to be inhabited. That is, emptiness was the initial stage, but not the final stage.[16] There were several stages in reaching the goal, each of them seen by God to be good because each of them had fulfilled the purpose God determined for it.

In any age readers of Genesis 1 would be familiar with

that most basic cycle of life, the human working week. They would also have known how the law of God in Exodus referred to the creation narrative: "Remember the Sabbath day, to keep it holy. Six days you shall labor, and do all your work, but the seventh day is a Sabbath to the LORD your God ... For in six days the Lord made heaven and earth, the sea, and all that is in them, and rested on the seventh day. Therefore the LORD blessed the Sabbath day and made it holy" (Exod. 20:8–11).

Thoughtful readers would therefore clearly understand the following: (1) Genesis 1 portrays God as a creative craftsman going about his week of work, taking rest each night from evening to morning and then having a day of rest at the end. (2) Yet God's work of creation was vastly different from human work. We do not do the things that God does. Indeed, the Hebrew word for "create" (*bara*) is used in the Bible only with God as subject. (3) Human rest is not the same as God's rest. God does not get tired as we do—he "neither slumbers nor sleeps" (Ps. 121:4). (4) God's creation week was never repeated, whereas that of the readers was. Thus there were points of contact between God's creation week and the readers' workweek that they could readily understand, and there were differences. They could see that the human workweek was similar to God's, but not identical. The question now is, how were the days of God's creation week to be understood?

THE MEANING OF THE WORD "DAY" IN GENESIS 1:1–2:4

1. The Hebrew word *yom*, "day," is first mentioned in Genesis 1:5: "God called the light Day, and the darkness he

called Night." What is the natural reading of this statement? Here day is contrasted with night; so a twenty-four-hour day is *not* in view, but rather "day" in the sense of "daytime"— roughly twelve hours. Compare John 11:9, where Jesus says, "Are there not twelve hours in the day?"[17] The words for "day" in New Testament Greek and in English, as well as Hebrew, have several primary meanings, and "daytime" is one of them.

2. The second time the word for "day" occurs, again in Genesis 1:5, it is in the context of saying that day one involves "evening and morning," and "day" would naturally then be understood to refer to a twenty-four-hour day. So now we have two primary meanings for the word "day" in the same verse.

3. The next occurrence of the word "day" that we need to pay attention to is in the account of the seventh day— the Sabbath, on which God rests from the work of creating. There is no mention here of "evening and morning," as there has been for each of the first six days. The omission is striking and calls for an explanation. If, for instance, we ask how long God rested from his work of creation, as distinct from his work of upholding the universe, then Augustine's suggestion, that God sanctified the seventh day by making it an epoch that extends onward into eternity, makes good sense; and this is followed by many commentators. Thus the seventh day is arguably different from the first six,[18] which are days of creative activity. The sequence of days comes to an end, and God rests from *creation* activity; and he is still resting up to this present day. That is, we are still today in God's Sabbath rest.[19] God is not, however, resting from all activity. In particular, he does not rest from the work of upholding the universe and the work of salvation

and redemption, as implied in Christ's statement when he was accused of breaking the Sabbath: "My Father is working until now, and I am working" (John 5:17).

It is this conviction, that the seventh day in the Genesis account is a long period of time, that leads some people to think that the other days may similarly be long ages. However, caution may be needed here since, as we have just seen, the text itself contains indications that day seven is different from the other six.

4. Finally, in some translations of Genesis 2:4 we meet the expression "When God created ..." In fact, the word "when" is used to translate the Hebrew for "in the day." Clearly the author has no more got a twenty-four-hour day in mind here than an elderly man would if he said, "In my day there were very few aircraft in the sky." He would be using the word "day" quite correctly to describe a period of time, not a particular day of a particular week. We might compare this use of the word with expressions like "the day of the LORD" and "the last day," which clearly refer to periods of undefined length, and not twenty-four-hour days.

The word "day," therefore, has several distinct meanings in the short text of Genesis 1:1 – 2:4 alone. Each of these meanings is familiar from ordinary usage. They are all natural, primary, "literal" meanings, each referring to something real and perfectly comprehensible.

A further grammatical point should be made. In many English versions of the Bible the days of Genesis are rendered as "*the* first day, *the* second day," and so on, each having the definite article. However, even though the Hebrew language does have a definite article (*ha*), it is not used in the original to qualify days one to five. Basil, a fourth-century bishop of

Caesarea, thought this significant: "If then the beginning of time is called 'one day' rather than 'the first day,' it is because Scripture wishes to establish its relationship with eternity. It was, in reality, fit and natural to call 'one' the day whose character is to be one wholly separated and isolated from all the others."[20] What is very striking is the additional fact pointed out to me by Old Testament scholar David Gooding: although the Hebrew definite article is not used with the first five days, *it is used for days six and seven*. A better translation, therefore, would be "day one, day two,..., day five, *the* sixth day, *the* seventh day"; or, "*a* first day, *a* second day,..., *the* sixth day, *the* seventh day."[21]

These then are the facts. The next question is, how should we interpret them?

THE NATURE OF THE CREATION WEEK

In the three-part structure of Genesis 1:1 – 2:3 mentioned above, the initial creation act (Gen.1:1 – 2) is separated from the six days of creation that follow it. You will find this structure followed, for instance, in the section in the ESV. The reason is that there is a clear pattern to the days: they each begin with the phrase "And God said" and end with the statement "and there was evening and there was morning, n^{th} day." This means that, according to the text, day 1 begins in verse 3 and not in verse 1. This is made clear in the original text by the fact that the verb "created" in Genesis1:1 is in the perfect tense, and "the normal use of the perfect at the very beginning of a pericope[22] is to denote an event that took place before the storyline gets under way."[23] The use of the narrative tense begins in verse 3.

This implies that "the beginning" of Genesis 1:1 did not necessarily take place on day 1 as is frequently assumed. The initial creation took place before day 1, but Genesis does not tell us how long before. This means that the question of the age of the earth (and of the universe) is a separate question from the interpretation of the days, a point that is frequently overlooked. In other words, quite apart from any scientific considerations, the text of Genesis 1:1, in separating the beginning from day 1, leaves the age of the universe indeterminate.

It would therefore be logically possible to believe that the days of Genesis are twenty-four-hour days (of one earth week) *and* to believe that the universe is very ancient. I repeat: this has nothing to do with science. Rather, it has to do with what the text actually says. There is a danger of understanding the text as saying less than it does, but also a danger of trying to make it say more.

The situation then is beginning to look similar to that of the fixed-earth controversy. There we saw that, although Scripture could be understood as teaching that the earth did not move, that was not the only logically possible interpretation. Here we see that, although Scripture could be understood as teaching that the earth is young, it does not have to be interpreted in this way.

Now for the days themselves. If we were listing the days of one normal earth week (in English), we would surely consistently give each of them either the indefinite article or leave articles out altogether. We would not, as Genesis does, remove the (definite) article from the first five days, and then supply it for the last two. The presence of the article indicates that the final two days are special: on the sixth day human beings are made in the image of God, and on the seventh God rests, his work complete.

This point of grammar may also be a signal to us that the text is rather more sophisticated than we might first have thought. In particular, it is often assumed that the writer of Genesis intended us to take the days *either* as seven days of one earth week (as in the twenty-four-hour view) *or* as seven time periods of indeterminate length (as in the day-age view) *or* as a logical framework in which to help us picture creation (as in the framework view).

However, there is another possibility: that the writer did not intend us to think of the first six days as days of a single earth week, but rather as a sequence of six *creation* days; that is, days of normal length (with evenings and mornings as the text says) in which God acted to create something new, but days that might well have been separated by long periods of time.[24] We have already seen that Genesis separates the initial creation, "the beginning," from the sequence of days. What we are now suggesting in addition is that the individual days might well have been separated from one another by unspecified periods of time.

On first hearing this, some of my readers will react negatively: "But isn't this rather far-fetched? Surely it goes against the natural, plain, straightforward reading of the text? In any case, isn't it clear that no reader in ancient times would ever have thought of it?"

I understand this objection very well, as it has also occurred to me; but I hope that, since you have been kind enough to journey with me this far, you will stretch your generosity to hear me out and reserve your judgement until you have reached the end of the discussion.

We are considering the idea that the six days encompass a sequence of creation acts, each of which involved at least one creative fiat[25] introduced by the phrase "And God said." This helps us understand what the New Testament means by saying that all things were made by the word of God. At each stage of creation God injected a new level of information and energy into the cosmos, in order to advance creation to its next level of form and complexity.[26] On this view, therefore, the six creation days themselves could well have been days of normal length, spaced out at intervals over the entire period of time that God took to complete his work. The outworking of the potential of each creative fiat would occupy an unspecified period of time after that particular creation day. One consequence of this is that we would expect to find what geologists tell us we do find—fossil evidence revealing the sudden appearance of new levels of complexity, followed by periods during which there was no more creation (in the sense of God speaking to inaugurate something radically new).[27]

The reader will have noticed that this view contains elements of each of the three dominant interpretations, but differs from each of them at particular points. It sees no difficulty with the six creation days being normal days as in the twenty-four-hour view, but it does not agree that they form a single earth week. It accepts the common day-age and framework view of the seventh day as a long period of time, but differs from those views for the first six days, in holding that each of the creation days *inaugurates* a period of outworking but is not coterminous with that period. It accepts the basic parallels between the first and second triads of days as in the framework view, but differs in that it does not take these parallels as disallowing a chronology implied by the succession of days, particularly with regard to days 1 and 4 (see below for a discussion of day 4).

An interesting variant on this theme, based on the common use of parentheses in literature in general and in the Bible in particular, has been suggested by Alan Hayward.[28] Parentheses are used to insert a separate, secondary thought into a passage or sentence in such a way that the sentence makes complete sense when read without the parenthetical remark. Here is an example from the New Testament: "In those days Peter stood up among the brothers (the company of persons was in all about 120) and said ..." (Acts 1:15).[29] We normally indicate parentheses by brackets (called parentheses in US usage), dashes, or quote marks, none of which existed in biblical times, although translators have often inserted them, as, for instance, in Genesis 2:5–7.

Hayward suggests that each of the first six days of Genesis involves a parenthesis. On this understanding, using brackets to indicate the parenthesis for clarity, day 1, for example, would read as follows: "And God said, 'Let there be light.' (And there was light. And God saw that the light was good. And God separated the light from the darkness. God called the light Day, and the darkness he called Night.) And there was evening and there was morning, the first day" (Gen. 1:3–5). According to this approach, Genesis 1:3–5 is "basically an account of the great creative fiats which were uttered upon the six (presumably literal, consecutive) days. Inserted into this primary narrative is a whole series of parentheses which describe the subsequent fulfilment of the fiats. The out-workings of the fiats, of course, could have taken any amount of time to occur. The fiats of God are uttered swiftly, but his mills grind slowly."[30]

Hayward goes on to argue that this interpretation helps us understand why the days of creation appear to be arranged in a formal manner (as per the framework view). It also explains why the order of events as recorded in Genesis bears a similarity to, but is not identical with, the order as deduced from the geological record: "The broad similarity is because the creative processes were presumably started in much the same order as the daily fiats. The discrepancies are because those creative processes took varying lengths of time to complete so that there would be a great deal of overlapping in the periods of active creation."[31]

I can imagine someone interrupting at this point, "But surely the answer is much simpler than this, and you have already referred to it when you quoted the law as saying, 'Six days you shall labor, and do all your work, but the seventh day is a Sabbath to the LORD your God ... For in six days the LORD made heaven and earth, the sea, and all that is in them, and rested the seventh day' (Exod. 20:9–11). Hence the days must surely be the days of a single earth week."

Yes, but when I mentioned this statement from the law, I pointed out that there were not only similarities between God's creation week and our work week, but also obvious differences. God's week happened once; ours is repeated. God's creative activity is very different from ours; God does not need rest as we do; and so on. So it is not possible to draw straight lines from Genesis to our working week. God's week is a pattern for ours, but it is not identical. Thus Exodus 20:8–11 does not *demand* that the days of Genesis 1 be the days of a single week, although it could of course be interpreted that way.

In light of this, C. John Collins has suggested another way of looking at the days that he calls the "analogical days view," a view that "takes the word [*day*] in its ordinary meaning, but applies that meaning analogically." He adds, "This is just what we do with other analogical terms like 'eyes of the Lord'; we don't need a new entry in the dictionary for 'eye'; we use the ordinary meaning and apply it by analogy to God."[32]

It would be a mistake, of course, to overemphasise the differences between some of the views mentioned in this chapter. No major doctrine of Scripture is affected by whether one believes that the days are analogical days or that each day is a long period of time inaugurated by God speaking, or whether one believes that each of the days is a normal day in which God spoke, followed by a long period of putting into effect the information contained in what God said on that particular day.[33]

THE PROBLEMATIC FOURTH DAY

We recall from above the point that Origen made long ago, which registers with many today. If there is a chronological dimension to the days, how is it that the sun was *made* on day 4? "And God said, "Let there be lights in the expanse of the heavens to separate the day from the night ... and let them be lights in the expanse of the heavens to give light upon the earth.' And it was so" (Gen. 1:14–15).

If the text means that the sun came into existence on day 4, Origen was asking a very reasonable question: "If the sun is not yet there, how are we to understand the first three days with their 'evenings and mornings'?" The word "day" makes no obvious sense in the absence of the sun and the earth's rotation relative to it. In order to overcome this difficulty, some have postulated the existence of a nonsolar light source that functioned for the first three days. However, apart from the fact that this would still leave the first three "days" undefined, we know nothing about such a light source, either from Scripture or from science.

The logical alternative is that the sun existed at the beginning of the Genesis week; and then the account of day 4 would have to be read in light of that fact. One suggestion is that on day 4 the sun, moon, and stars *appeared* as distinguishable lights in the sky when the cloud cover that had concealed them dissipated.[34]

However, from a linguistic perspective C. John Collins suggests a third possibility: "The verb 'made' in Genesis 1:16 does not specifically mean 'create'; it can refer to that, but it can also refer to 'working on something that is already there' (hence ESV margin), or even 'appointed.'"[35] Indeed, this interpretation fits well with the explanation, given in the very next verse, of the function of the sun and moon as visible lights in the sky. That is, the verse is speaking about God appointing the role of the sun and moon in the cosmos, and not speaking of either their creation or their appearing.[36]

The framework view handles Origen's interpretive problem by suggesting that day 4 covers exactly the same ground as day 1, but from a different perspective. In day 1 it is said, "And God separated the light from the darkness. God called the light Day, and the darkness he called Night" (1:4–5). On day 4 God says, "Let there be lights in the expanse of the heavens to separate the day from the night ... and God made the two great lights" (1:14–16). Thus, in the framework view, day 4 does not follow day 1 chronologically, but rather revisits day 1 with details of how God separated day and night by means of sun and moon. One obvious problem with this is that it effectively reduces the number of the days to three instead of six in a rather unnatural way that loses the parallel with the human workweek given in Exodus 20:9–11.

In any case, the fact that some early church fathers had difficulties with interpreting the text should give us some comfort, make us more humble, and, in addition, show us that the difficulties are not all generated by modern science but arise from a serious attempt to understand the text itself.

A COMMON OBJECTION

Finally, I have not forgotten the common objection to what I have been saying in this chapter—that it is contrived to make Scripture subservient to science, since no one could have arrived at these sophisticated interpretations in the ancient world.

This is a reasonable objection, and I take it seriously. At the very least the second point is clearly justified. Let me respond by saying first that what I have tried to do so far is to look at what the text of Genesis actually says, irrespective of any scientific considerations, and in light of that to consider possible interpretations.

If you say that these seem contrived to fit in with science, I would point out that this is not the first time that such a question has arisen. Indeed, it is for that very reason that I wrote chapter 1. We saw there that the same kind of issue arose half a millennium ago, not in connection with the age of the earth or the days of Genesis but with the motion of the earth.

In that chapter we found that understanding the foundations and pillars of the earth as referring to the stability of the earth is not a compromise position, but a perfectly reasonable understanding of the text that does not undermine the authority of Scripture, even though this interpretation relies on (new) scientific knowledge.

What we need to grasp is that this is a perfectly normal way of approaching such matters. We all use it every day. For instance, earlier we discussed the interpretation of the statement "the car is flying down the road" and Jesus' statement "I am the door." What is it that helps us to understand that both statements are to be taken metaphorically and not literalistically? It is our experience of the world. We do this so habitually, of course, that we are usually unaware of it. It involves in essence a simple reality check: does our interpretation make sense in the real world? So, regarding science informally as organised knowledge inferred from experience of the world around us, we see that science helps us to decide what meaning to go for in both of the examples given.

This helps us to answer the objection that we must interpret the Genesis days as twenty-four-hour days of a single earth week, since that is what most people thought for centuries. If we applied that kind of reasoning to the interpretation of the foundations and pillars of the earth, then we would still be insisting that the earth does not move. Yet I have never met a young-earth creationist who thinks that way. What we learn from this is that it is just not adequate to choose an interpretation simply on the basis of asking how many people held this interpretation, and for how long.[37]

One has to ask why they understood it that way at that time, and one also has to ask if there are compelling reasons for changing that understanding. In the case of the motion of the earth there were reasons for changing the interpretation that are now clear and settled. The lesson for us is that we need to be prepared to apply the same kind of thinking to the age of the earth.

The following comment on the moving-earth controversy by a leading young-earth creationist is noteworthy: "Only when such a position became mathematically and observationally 'hopeless,' should the church have abandoned it. This is in fact what the church did. Young earth creationism, therefore, need not embrace a dogmatic or static biblical hermeneutic. It must be willing to change and admit error. Presently, we can admit that as recent creationists we are defending a very natural biblical account, at the cost of abandoning a very plausible scientific picture of an 'old' cosmos. *But over the long term this is not a tenable position.* In our opinion, old earth creationism combines a less natural textual reading with a much more plausible scientific vision ... At the moment this would seem the more rational position to adopt."[38]

The major thrust of my argument so far, then, is that there is a way of understanding Genesis 1 that does not compromise the authority and primacy of Scripture and that, at the same time, takes into account our increased knowledge of the universe, as Scripture itself suggests we should (Rom. 1:19–20).

However, some of my readers will object that I have not mentioned the theological problems associated with believing in an ancient earth, problems that arise not so much in

Genesis 1 but in the subsequent chapters. They are quite right. In particular, I have not yet discussed the matter of the entry of death into the world. We must now look at this important issue in the context of what Genesis says about the origin of humanity.

NOTES

1. Calvin wrote: "Here the error of those is manifestly refuted, who maintain that the world was made in a moment. For it is too violent a cavil to contend that Moses distributes the work which God perfected at once into six days, for the mere purpose of conveying instruction. Let us rather conclude that God himself took the space of six days, for the purpose of accommodating his works to the capacity of men." *Commentaries on the first book of Moses, called Genesis* (Grand Rapids: Eerdmans, 1948), chap. 1, v. 5, p. 78.

2. Irenaeus, *Irenaeus Against Heresies,* book V, in Alexander Roberts and James Donaldson, *Ante-Nicene Christian Library: Translations of the Writings of the Gathers down to A.D. 325,* vol. IX (Edinburgh: T&T Clark), 118.

3. Alexander Roberts and James Donaldson, *Ante-Nicene Christian Library: Translations of the Writings of the Gathers down to A.D. 325,* vol. II (New York: Charles Scribner's Sons, 1899), 513.

4. G. W. Butterworth (tr.), *Origen on First Principles* (Gloucester: Peter Smith, 1973), 288.

5. Augustine, *The City of God: Writings of Saint Augustine,* vol. 14 (Ann Arbor: University of Michigan/Fathers of the Church, 1947), 196.

6. A very useful discussion of this issue appears in C. John Collins, *Genesis 1–4: A Linguistic, Literary, and Theological Commentary* (Phillipsburg, NJ: P&R, 2006), 13ff.

7. In appendix A we discuss some relevant material from the surrounding ancient empires of Egypt, Assyria, and Mesopotamia.

8. In appendix B we consider one particularly influential example of the argument that the Genesis cosmology is culturally relative.

9. For interactive discussions of the main views by well-known representatives, see David G. Hagopian, ed., *The Genesis Debate: Three Views on the Days of Creation* (Mission Viejo, CA: Crux Press, 2001), and J. P. Moreland and John Mark Reynolds, eds., *Three Views of Creation and Evolution* (Grand Rapids: Zondervan, 1999).

10. J. G. von Herder, *The Spirit of Hebrew Poetry*, trans. James Marsh (Burlington, Ontario: Edward Smith, 1833), 1:58. See also Gordon J. Wenham, *Genesis 1–15*, Word Biblical Commentary (Waco, TX: Word Books, 1987), 6–7. See also various sources cited in Hagopian, *The Genesis Debate*.

11. See David W. Gooding, *According to Luke* (Leicester, UK: Inter-Varsity, 1987).

12. John Walton, *The Lost World of Genesis One* (Downers Grove, IL: InterVarsity, 2009), 92. For more detail see appendix B.

13. This point has also been made by biblical languages expert Dr. Peter Williams, Warden of Tyndale House, Cambridge University. For a discussion of whether the use of literary symmetry can be consistent with historicity, see Gooding, *According to Luke,* 358.

14. Derek Kidner, *Genesis* (Leicester, UK: Tyndale Press, 1967), 54–55.

15. Collins, *Genesis 1–4*, 74.

16. Isaiah 45:18. This is surely a more natural way to read the text than taking it to indicate that the "empty" state of the earth was the result of some great catastrophe, which occurred, so to speak, between verses 1 and 2 of Genesis 1. There is no indication that being "without form and void" is in itself a bad thing.

17. We shall come back to the meaning of this statement in chap. 5.

18. This is accepted by both the day-age view and the framework view.

19. See Heb. 4:3–11.

20. Basil adds that "if Scripture speaks to us of many ages, saying everywhere 'ages of ages,' we do not see it enumerate them as first, second, and third. It follows that we are hereby shown not so much limits, ends, and successions of ages, as distinctions between various states and modes of action." P. Schaff and H. Wace, *A Select Library of Nicene and Post-Nicene Fathers of the Christian Church: St. Basil:*

Letters and Select Works, vol. VIII, 2nd series (New York: Christian Literature Company, 1895), 64.

21. This, according to scholars, is a possible translation, although Hebrew does not have an equivalent for the English indefinite article *a/an.*

22. A technical word for a section or short passage from a book (from the Greek meaning "to cut around").

23. Collins, *Genesis 1–4,* 51.

24. A variant of this view is given by Robert Newman and Herman Ecklemann, who suggest that each day opens a new creative period (*Genesis One and the Origin of the Earth* [Leicester, UK: Inter-Varsity Press, 1977], 64–65). See also Newman's chapter "Progressive Creationism," in J. P. Moreland and John Mark Reynolds, eds., *Three Views on Creation and Evolution* (Grand Rapids: Zondervan, 1999), 105–33.

25. *Fiat* is Latin for "Let there be," as in "Fiat Lux," which means "Let there be light." On days 3 and 6 there is more than one such expression.

26. Note that this is very different from what is suggested by mainstream evolutionary theory. See appendix E and also Lennox, *God's Undertaker,* for further details.

27. Microevolutionary processes of the uncontroversial kind that we observe would have been part of the outworking and settling-down period after each creation day.

28. Alan Hayward, *Creation and Evolution* (London: SPCK, 1987), 169.

29. See also the longer parenthesis formed by Acts 1:18–19.

30. Hayward, *Creation and Evolution,* 170–71.

31. Ibid., 176–77.

32. C. John Collins, *Science and Faith* (Wheaton: Crossway, 2003), 95.

33. That is, unless one thinks, as some do, that the length of the days is itself one of those major doctrines.

34. Hugh Ross, amongst others, has made this suggestion, in The Genesis Question, 2nd expanded ed. (Colorado Springs: Navpress, 2001), 43. On this view, the earth started hot (as in the standard Hot Big Bang model of physics), and so the sun, even though it had

existed from the start, would not have been visible from earth until the earth had cooled sufficiently to allow the cloud cover to thin and disperse. An observer could have seen the light of the sun but not its source. Also, it is not necessary for the sun to be visible for its light and heat to facilitate the maintenance of life's processes.

35. Collins, *Science and Faith*, 57.

36. A point strongly emphasized in Walton's cosmic temple view.

37. Although, of course, it is always important to take note of what people in other times have thought.

38. Moreland and Reynolds, *Three Views of Creation and Evolution*, 73 (emphasis added). I am not myself convinced that the old-earth reading is less natural than the young-earth reading, if we are simply thinking in terms of the age of the earth. The reason for this is that since, as we saw earlier in this chapter, the text of Genesis 1 separates the initial creation from the first day, the age of the earth is a logically separate matter from the nature of the days.

CHAPTER FOUR

HUMAN BEINGS: A SPECIAL CREATION?

THERE IS PROBABLY more controversy today over the origin of human beings than there is over the origin of the universe; and so no discussion of the creation week would be complete without saying something about the origin of humanity. After all, the making of human beings is the pinnacle of God's creation activity, and it has deep significance for our understanding of what we and our fellow men and women are. Genesis says that human beings are special: "So God created man in his own image, in the image of God he created him; male and female he created them" (Gen. 1:27).

Jesus himself put the stamp of his divine authority on the creation of humankind. In his discussion with the Pharisees about marriage and divorce, he said, "Have you not read that he who created them from the beginning made them male and female, and said, 'Therefore a man shall leave his father and his mother and hold fast to his wife, and the two shall become one flesh'? So they are no longer two but one flesh. What therefore God has joined together, let not man separate" (Matt. 19:4–6; see also Mark 10:6–9). Jesus draws attention to the fact these were the very words of the Creator himself: "He who created them ... *said*."

This is an immensely important reminder of the value, indeed the sacredness, of the marital bond in a world that is increasingly guilty of devaluing it. We men and women desperately need to heed this voice from Genesis in order to avoid the disintegration of our social fabric. For centuries, in the West at least, this biblical teaching has been the foundation of moral values, legislation, and human rights; but it is coming under increasing attack, not only by scientists but also by leading ethicists building on what scientists have to say. Peter Singer of Princeton University, for example, one of the most influential contemporary ethicists, writes:

> Whatever the future holds, it is likely to prove impossible to restore in full the sanctity-of-life view. The philosophical foundations of this view have been knocked asunder. We can no longer base our ethics on the idea that human beings are a special form of creation made in the image of God, singled out from all other animals, and alone possessing an immortal soul. Our better understanding of our own nature has bridged the gulf that was once thought to lie between ourselves and other species, so why should we believe that the mere fact that a being is a member of the species Homo Sapiens endows its life with some unique, almost infinite value?[1]

In a similar vein, John Gray, Emeritus Professor of the History of European Thought at the London School of Economics, says that, over the past two hundred years, philosophy "has not given up Christianity's cardinal error — the belief that humans are radically different from other animals."[2]

The claimed science base for this is, of course, the theory of evolution. Hence the ethical arguments depend not only on the validity and reach of evolutionary theory in biological terms, but also on the validity of philosophical extrapolations and deductions from it.[3] I wish to comment here on the biblical view, and its implications in this connection.

Of all creation, only humans are made in God's image. "The heavens declare the glory of God" (Ps. 19:1), and there is nothing like a night under the magnificent canopy of the stars, in a remote part of the country that is free from light pollution, to convince one of this (especially if one has a telescope or binoculars). However, we never read in Scripture that the heavens bear the image of God. Only humans do.

Genesis does not deny what chemistry tells us — that all life has a material substrate of common elements. In Genesis 1:11 this fact is implied for vegetation and animals: "let the earth sprout vegetation"; and also in 1:24: "let the earth bring forth living creatures." In Genesis 2:7 it is explicitly said of humans, "the LORD God formed the man of dust from the ground and breathed into his nostrils the breath of life, and the man became a living creature." Therefore Genesis affirms that (human) life has a chemical base, but Genesis denies the reductionist addendum of the materialist — that life is nothing but chemistry.

Moreover, in saying that God made man of the dust of the ground, Genesis seems to be going out of its way to imply a direct special creation act, rather than suggesting that humans arose, either by natural processes or by God's special activity, out of preexisting hominids or, indeed, Neolithic farmers.[4]

The New Testament supports this understanding of a special creation of man. Firstly, the genealogy[5] of Jesus given in Luke tracks backwards to "Adam, the son of God" (Luke 3:38). Secondly, Jesus, in his famous discourse on marriage, says, "But from the beginning of creation, 'God made them male and female'" (Mark 10:6). Thirdly, Paul explicitly mentions the making of man from the dust of the ground: "The first man was from the earth, a man of dust; the second man is from heaven" (1 Cor. 15:47).

We have already noted that the yawning gulf between inorganic and organic matter is underlined in Genesis by the fact that on day 3 God spoke twice. This feature also characterises day 6, when God also speaks more than once: the first time to say, "Let the earth bring forth living creatures …" and the second, "Let us make man …"

This, surely deliberate, repetition is a clear indicator that, according to Genesis, you cross neither the gulf between nonlife and life nor the gulf between animals and human beings by unguided natural processes. God has to speak his creative Word in both instances. Without God speaking there is an unbridgeable discontinuity. The image of God in man was not produced as a result of blind matter fumbling its unguided way through myriad different permutations. Thus Genesis challenges atheism's fundamental assertion that human life has appeared without the activity of God's mind, so that there is nothing special about human beings. I am tempted to add that it looks as if the writer of Genesis foresaw the contemporary debate!

The difference between animals and humans is further underscored by the fact that God assigned to humans the responsibility of stewardship "over" the animals (Gen. 1:26). Finally, that difference is also the focus in Genesis 2:18–24, where the way in which the narrative is structured shows that the naming of the animals is to be read in the context of finding a helper for Adam. The lesson is that there was no helper found fit for (or, corresponding to) Adam among the many animal species then existing (therefore, including, be it noted, nonhuman hominids). It is interesting that the first lesson Adam was taught, according to the Bible, is that he was fundamentally different from *all* other creatures.

Furthermore, the main thrust[6] of the Genesis account of the creation of woman from man seems to provide little support for the suggestion, made by biologist Denis Alexander amongst others, not only that there were millions of other humans at the time, but also that Eve was one of them.[7] Alexander does not deny (as many do) the historicity of Adam and Eve. However, it is the nature of his historical understanding that I find difficult to square with the biblical account. His preferred model of events (called Model C) is that Adam and Eve were two Neolithic farmers out of all the millions produced by the evolutionary process. God chose these two "to start his new spiritual family on earth, consisting of all who put their trust in God by faith, expressed in obedience to his will."[8] There is no physical dimension in this understanding of the Genesis creation account: "Just as I can go out on the streets of Cambridge today and have no idea just by looking at people, all of them members of the species *Homo sapiens*, which ones are spiritually alive, so in Model C there was no physical way of distinguishing between Adam and Eve and their contemporaries. It is a model about spiritual life and revealed commands and responsibilities, not about genetics."[9]

We read many times in Genesis, as well as in the rest of the Bible, that God chooses to reveal himself spiritually to human beings in a special way—Noah, Abraham, Isaac, and Jacob, for example. However, when Genesis speaks of God revealing himself to human beings, it uses the appropriate language. For instance, "The LORD appeared to Abram."[10] The creation account does not use such language; for Genesis 1 and 2 are not talking about God revealing himself to humans that already existed, but rather explaining how those human beings came to exist in the first place. The text is not describing the calling of existing human beings into fellowship with God, but stating how God physically created human beings from the dust of the earth in order to have fellowship with him. Moreover, the Genesis narrative makes it evident that Adam and Eve did not need to be called into fellowship with God at the beginning: they were in fellowship with God from the start. It was their sin that broke the fellowship.

Alexander goes on to say, "The text of Genesis 1 makes clear that the whole of humankind without any exception is made in God's image, including certainly all the other millions of people alive in the world in Neolithic times and since."[11] If, however, all human beings that were alive before and at the time of Adam and Eve bore the image of God, then the account of the creation of human beings "in God's image" recorded in Genesis 1 is very different from the story of Adam and Eve in Genesis 2, and indeed must have happened long before it.

What was that event, then, that conferred God's image on the whole of humankind? And what does Alexander mean when he says that Genesis 2 places "the creation of *adam* at the beginning of creation"?[12] His interpretation becomes even more difficult to follow when we put the biblical statement "there was *no* man to *work the ground*" (Gen. 2:5; emphasis added) alongside his suggestion that there were millions of Neolithic *farmers* in existence at the time.

Alexander also says, "Religious beliefs existed before this time, as *people* sought after God or gods in different parts of the world."[13] I presume that Alexander thinks that these people were moral beings (otherwise they would not be fully human). If this is the case, it is hard to imagine that there was neither human sin nor human death in the world in the time before God chose to reveal himself to a particular pair. It then becomes difficult to make sense of the biblical teaching that "sin came into the world through one man, and death through sin, and so death spread to all men" (Rom. 5:12). How, for example, could the sin of the chosen farmer, Adam, cause the death of those humans who had lived before him? Surely it is crucial to the theology of salvation that Adam was the first actual member of a human race physically distinct from all creatures that preceded him?

Furthermore, in one of the curious ironies of evolutionary theory, Alexander argues that human evolution has stopped.[14] Might not the true situation be that it never got started in the first place — that human beings were a direct creation of God?[15]

For the Christian, another consideration bears on this question of the uniqueness of human beings. The central claim of Christianity is, "The Word became flesh and dwelt among us" (John 1:14). God coded himself into humanity. He became a man. There is no question as to this being the central supernatural event in history—a direct action of God of unfathomable significance.

In light of the miracle of the incarnation, I find no difficulty in believing that the human race itself began—indeed, had to begin—with a supernatural intervention. Science cannot rule out that possibility either.[16] What science can tell about human beings, though, is what it can tell us about the universe: that they also had a beginning. What the incarnation tells us is that human beings are unique—they are so created that God himself could become one.

THE ANTIQUITY OF HUMANITY

We referred earlier to Archbishop Ussher's calculations regarding the age of the earth. Ussher regarded the days of creation as days of one earth week. Taking the beginning of that week as the creation of the earth, and the end of the week as the starting point for humanity, Ussher used the genealogies given in Genesis to complete his calculation of the age of the earth. His calculation was therefore intimately linked with his estimate of the age of humanity. Our discussion of Genesis up to this point has been concerned with the nature of the days in Genesis 1, and not with questions about the antiquity of humanity.

Regarding calculations made with the use of genealogies, Kitchen points out, "Within Hebrew and related tradition, such 'official' father-to-son sequences can represent the actual facts of life, or they can be a condensation from an originally longer series of generations."[17] He gives example from Genesis, where lists of sons included grandsons and great-grandsons, and also points out that in the genealogy given in Matthew 1:8, the statement "Jehoram [was] the father of Uzziah" is shorthand for "Jehoram was the father of Ahaziah, who was the father of Joash, who was the father of Amaziah, who was the father of Uzziah." Thus he concludes that in Genesis 1–11, "we see the narrative in some cases presupposing immediate fatherhood.... But in most cases, one may in principle as easily read the recurring formulae 'A fathered B, and after fathering B lived x years,' as 'A fathered (the line culminating in) B, and after fathering (the line culminating in) B, lived x years.'"[18]

Thus, on the internal evidence of Scripture, the dating of the age of humanity is indeterminate. However, it is important not to confuse things that differ, namely, the age of the universe, the age of the earth, the age of life, and the age of humanity. Clearly, the earth is younger than the universe, biological life is younger than the earth, and human life is younger than biological life.

A THEOLOGICAL OBJECTION: DEATH BEFORE ADAM'S SIN?

The idea that the earth may have existed long before the creation of human beings creates a theological problem — the existence of death before the entry of sin into the world. This matter arises because of the statement of St. Paul: "Therefore, just as sin came into the world through one man, and death through sin, and so death spread to all men because all sinned ..." (Rom. 5:12). The argument is simply that, since death is a consequence of human sin, no death could have occurred before man sinned. This is clearly a serious issue with profound implications for the doctrine of salvation, since, as has often been pointed out, if Paul is wrong in his diagnosis of the origin of sin and death, how can we expect him to be right regarding its solution?

I am now faced with an additional problem. In a short introductory book, as this is intended to be, concentrating mainly on the time of creation, it is simply impossible to include a detailed discussion of the nature and provenance of the events described in Genesis 3, immensely important though that is. So I shall have to content myself (and thus risk discontenting some readers!) with sketching some of the ideas that seem to me to bear directly on the question as stated above.

The Genesis account of the entry of sin into the world (Gen. 3:1–7) is one of the most fascinating parts of the Bible. The action takes place in the Garden of Eden and has to do with its plants, animals, and humans, or, more accurately, with a special tree, the Tree of the Knowledge of Good and Evil; a special animal, the serpent; and, of course, Adam and Eve.

The first humans have been placed in the garden and told that they may eat of every tree (including by implication that other special tree, the Tree of Life) except for the Tree of the Knowledge of Good and Evil. They are warned that if they eat of this tree, they will die. That is, they have the capacity to eat of all of the trees without exception, but not the permission to eat of one particular tree. Here the basic ingredients that define human beings as moral beings. God has given them the ability to say "yes" to him by not eating the prohibited tree, and to say "no" to him by eating it. In this way the Bible introduces us to the idea that the humans are moral beings, with all that this implies.

We are next introduced to one of the chief actors in the drama—the serpent. We are told that it "was more crafty than any other beast of the field that the LORD God had made" (3:1). It turns out to be very different from the other creatures: it is clever and it can speak. It engages Eve in conversation about the significance of eating the prohibited Tree of the Knowledge of Good and Evil. It first questions the prohibition: "Did God actually say, 'You shall not eat of any tree in the garden'?" (3:1). Eve answers, rather inaccurately, by saying that God has forbidden even touching the tree, let alone eating it. The serpent responds with outright denial: "You will not surely die." To this the serpent adds, "God knows that when you eat of it your eyes will be opened, and you will be like God, knowing good and evil" (3:5).

The serpent contrives, by a devious manipulation of half-truth and a subtle appeal to her (God-given) interest in food, her aesthetic sense, and her desire for insight and fulfilment, to drive a wedge between her and her Creator. The snake's power of persuasion is such that Eve takes the forbidden fruit[19] and offers it to Adam, and they both eat.

In that searing moment they discover that the enlightenment received is far from what they thought they desired. Instead of finding life, they begin to experience death, as God had said they would. They do not at once die in the physical sense: that effect of their action will inevitably ensue in due course. Human life, as we learn from Genesis 2, has many aspects; its lowest level is physical life, to which we must add those other things that make life life—aesthetic environment, work, human relationships, and a relationship with God. Human death, then, will involve the unweaving of all of this: it will first mean the death of fellowship with God, and the first result of this death is a pathetic attempt to hide from God in the garden. The deadly rupture of fellowship with God will then lead inexorably to all the other levels of death—aesthetic death, death of human relationships, and so on, until we reach the lowest level of death, which turns our bodies back to molecules of dust.

With this all too brief sketch we turn to see exactly what Paul says about it—and what he does not say. He says that death passed upon all *human beings* as a result of Adam's sin; he does not say that death passed upon *all living things*. That is, what Scripture actually says is that *human* death is a consequence of sin.[20] That makes sense. Humans are moral beings, and human death is the ultimate wages of moral transgression. We do not think of plants and animals in terms of moral categories. We do not accuse the lion of sinning when it kills an antelope or even a human being. Paul's deliberate and careful statement would appear to leave open the question of death at levels other than human.

Indeed, since fruit and vegetables[21] are explicitly mentioned as (God-given) diet in Genesis, plant life can scarcely be an issue here. Plant death cannot therefore have been a consequence of the first human sin, even though plant death is death. What about the animals? Whales, for instance, are mammals, and they do not live on green vegetation. Their food is living sea-food; and so, by eating, whales cause death.

The same is true of many sea and land creatures. Had they some alternative source of food before Adam sinned? Hardly.

In a similar way, the view that animal death did not exist before humans sinned makes the existence of predators problematic. The woodpecker has astonishingly powerful muscles in its neck to enable it to peck out insects. Some snakes secrete poisons, and some fish can launch bolts of electricity that stun their prey. Furthermore, many animals and fish have camouflage systems to avoid predation: there are insects that look poisonous to birds even though they aren't actually poisonous. If there was no death of any kind before the first human sin (and therefore no predation), did these exquisitely complex neck muscles, poison sacs, electrical organs, and camouflage systems come into existence as a result of that sin? If that is so, would it not make that sin the trigger of a creation process — a feature that seems very unlikely, and on which the Bible appears to be silent? Or did God foresee the change, build the mechanisms into the creatures in advance, and then do something to set them in operation?

I begin to think that Occam's Razor[22] may need to be applied at this point in order to restrict the multiplication of unnecessary hypotheses — that is, if the theological problem arises from going beyond what Paul actually says.

Now, the question will at once arise as to what Paul then means by his later statement: "For the creation was subjected to futility, not willingly, but because of him who subjected it, in hope that the creation itself will be set free from its bondage to corruption and obtain the freedom of the glory of the children of God" (Rom. 8:20 – 21). Surely, it will be said, this must mean that all death is a result of human sin?

Once more we need to observe exactly what is being said. Paul speaks of decay and corruption. Think of what happens to flowers. Daffodils can get disease. However, daffodils, whether diseased or not, die down in the early summer. Only the bulbs are left, which then grow again the following year. Is that process of dying down the same thing as disease? Surely not. It is part of what we call the cycle of nature. Is this a good thing, part of the original creation, or is it a result of sin? Similarly, salmon can become diseased. But that is not the same thing as salmon dying after they have spawned. Once more, this strange phenomenon is part of the cycle of nature. Again, is this a good thing, or is it a result of sin?

Is it therefore possible that corruption, disease, and human death may well be a consequence of sin, but that plant and animal death, as part of the cycle of nature, are not?[23] One might then reasonably argue that Romans 8:20–21 is carefully written to refer to decay and corruption as distinct from death. Once more the key is to observe exactly what Scripture says.

It is also helpful to think about the circumstances in which human death was introduced into the world. We are told that there was a Tree of Life in the garden, to which free access was granted (Gen. 2:16). One consequence of Adam's sin was that access to that tree was barred, "'lest he reach out his hand and take also of the tree of life and eat, and live forever'—therefore the LORD God sent him out from the Garden of Eden" (Gen. 3:22–23). This could mean, as many think, that Adam had never eaten of it and God was grateful he hadn't. But could it not also mean that this special food was near him while he was in the garden, so that all he needed to do was put forth his hand to take it? Once he was outside the garden, he could no longer do that, since the tree was only in one place, the middle of the garden.[24]

This leads to the question, at creation did human beings have essential, inherent immortality that was removed when they sinned? Or, in light of the New Testament's explicit statement, "[God] alone has immortality" (1 Tim. 6:16), does it follow that Adam never had intrinsic immortality, but was dependent from the beginning on regular access to an external source of food (the Tree of Life) for continued existence?

The relevance of this to the question of nonhuman death is simply this: what was the status of other living creatures, for example animals and birds, with respect to the Tree of Life? Did they have intrinsic immortality or not? If they had (which might be somewhat surprising if humans didn't), what did God subsequently do to remove that immortality, as distinct from what he did to man? There is no mention of removing birds and animals from the garden. On the other hand, if the animals and birds were also dependent on the tree of life, what about those animals and birds that were, presumably, outside the garden from the beginning? From the biblical text one does not get the impression that the entire world was like Eden. Indeed the very opposite seems to be implied by the statement that God planted a garden. That raises even more questions: what was the difference, exactly, between the inside and the outside of that garden? When we think of gardens we tend to think only of the plants, but in the account of the Garden of Eden there is clear interest in the animals as well as the plants. What, then, was the situation of not only the flora but the fauna outside the idyllic Garden of Eden? We can only speculate.

Whatever the answers are to these questions, it would seem that Scripture itself leaves open the possibility that animals died before sin entered the world without affecting the fact that human death was a consequence of that sin.[25]

This should not be taken to mean, however, that I think that I have solved all the questions that arise here. In particular, two things spring at once to mind. The first is that, where does animal *pain* fit into all of this? For, it will be said, if predation is part of the cycle of nature, how can that be a good thing when, as we are increasingly aware, it is frequently attended by the most horrific suffering on the part of the victims? Was there, for instance, a difference between the behaviour of animals outside the Garden of Eden and that of those in the idyllic situation inside? If so, what was the cause?

That brings me to the second thing — the role of the snake in the entry of sin into the world. What was this serpent whose insinuations triggered such a seismic catastrophe, from which the world has been reeling ever since? It appears unannounced on the page of Genesis, simply described as one of the creatures that God had made. But that is already telling us something — and simultaneously raising many questions. For this serpent is a creature; so God is ultimately responsible for its existence. Yet it is clearly opposed to God. In other words, Genesis is saying that there was already an alien in the earth, a being that, apparently, had the capacity to disobey God, had done so, and was now encouraging the first humans to follow suit.

Now some people will dismiss all of this as primitive mythology. I do not. Indeed, I find it rather ironic that many people who summarily reject this account as having nothing to do with reality are perfectly prepared to accept without question the verdict of scientists who inform them that the universe must be teeming with extraterrestrial life (even though they have not as yet discovered evidence of its existence).

There are other reasons to be sceptical of the mythological view. For instance, according to Genesis, God pronounced sentence on the serpent for what it had done: "Because you have done this, cursed are you above all livestock and above all beasts of the field; on your belly you shall go, and dust you shall eat all the days of your life. I will put enmity between you and the woman, and between your offspring and her offspring; he shall bruise your head, and you shall bruise his heel" (Gen. 3:14–15). The first part of the punishment is that the serpent will henceforth slither on the ground—the implication being that we are talking of an actual creature that previously stood upright. Secondly, the serpent is to have offspring opposed to the offspring of the woman. But one particular offspring of the woman will triumph over the serpent by bruising his head.

The rest of Genesis will be the first part of the story of the offspring (or seed) of the woman, a story that will reach its climax in the Offspring or Seed, Jesus Christ. The New Testament is not embarrassed to say that Christ is opposed not only by human malevolence but by a nonhuman, supernatural being, the enemy himself, the devil, who is called Satan, the Accuser. Now Genesis 3 does not use any of these words, but it is not hard to see from subsequent Scripture that behind the serpent described in that chapter there is the malevolent figure of the devil—"that ancient serpent," as he is called in the last book of the Bible, Revelation (12:9; 20:2). Indeed, many of the concepts in Genesis 3 come together once again in the drama of Revelation, where we read of a talking beast that is energised by the power of the devil, has worldwide authority (13:4–7), and is finally overcome by Christ himself (19:20).

Now, however intriguing all of this may be, we cannot divert into further discussion of it. I simply wish to make the point that, according to Scripture, evil in the universe appears to antedate the sin of Adam and Eve. C. S. Lewis puts it this way:

> It is impossible at this point not to remember a certain sacred story which, though never included in the creeds, has been widely believed in the Church and seems to be implied in several Dominical, Pauline and Johannine utterances — I mean the story that man was not the first creature to rebel against the Creator, but that some older, mightier being long since became apostate and is now the emperor of darkness and (significantly) the Lord of this world.[26]

Lewis goes on to say,

> It seems to me, therefore, a reasonable supposition, that some mighty created power had already been at work for ill on the material universe, or the solar system, or, at least, the planet Earth, before ever man came on the scene; and that when man fell, someone had, indeed tempted him ... If there is such a power, as I myself believe, it may well have corrupted the animal creation before man appeared.[27]

One thing at least is clear from Genesis: that dark power had corrupted at least part of the animal creation. Could it be that this is the direction in which we must look in order to begin to comprehend the origin of the pain and suffering that seems to permeate the animal kingdom?

The question of the origin of humans—are we made in the image of God, or thrown up on the sea of the possible random permutations of matter without any ultimate significance?—is of major importance for our concept of our human identity; and it is therefore not surprising that ferocious efforts are being made to minimise the difference between humans and animals on the one hand, and the difference between humans and machines on the other. Such efforts are driven, at least in part, by the secular conviction that naturalism must in the end triumph over theism by its reductionist arguments in removing the last vestige of God from his creation. Human beings must in the end be proved to be nothing but physics and chemistry.

It is important therefore to combat that naturalism by presenting biblical theism as a credible alternative that, far from involving intellectual suicide, makes more sense of the data than does atheistic reductionism.

THE WAY FORWARD

We have seen how the change from a fixed-earth to a moving-earth interpretation of Scripture came about as a result of gradually increasing scientific evidence that the earth was in motion. The parallel evidence regarding the antiquity of the universe is more recent, coming to us first from the disciplines of geology and most recently from advances in astronomy and cosmology. Of course I am well aware that the biological theory of evolution demands an ancient earth, and for many people this is a major factor in their thinking. However, the cosmological evidence is completely independent of biology, and it is therefore perfectly possible to accept that cosmological evidence without committing oneself to the belief that life has arisen by an unguided materialistic evolutionary process. It is simply false to suggest, as some do, that the only alternative to young-earth creationism is to accept the Darwinian model. I have discussed this and other related issues in my book *God's Undertaker*, and have also devoted appendix E in this book to the question of theistic evolution.

Now all true scientists are aware, of course, that science is not infallible: theories change (for example, as we have seen regarding the motion of the earth). Most scientists, though, are critical realists. They believe that they are making steps towards grasping the truth about the universe, but they are prepared to modify their theories if the evidence warrants it. We Christians need to remind ourselves of the two dangers outlined at the end of chapter 2. Firstly, we must beware of tying our exposition of Scripture so close to science that the former falls if the latter changes. On the other hand, we would be very unwise to ignore science through obscurantism or fear, and present to the world an image of a Christianity that is anti-intellectual. No Christian has anything to fear from true science. Many Christians have made, and continue to make, first-rate contributions to science.

So what is the best way forward? There seem to me to be four salient considerations:

The current scientific evidence for an ancient earth.

The honest and admirable admission of prominent young-earth creationists that "recent creationists should humbly agree that their view is, at the moment, implausible on purely scientific grounds. They can make common cause with those who reject naturalism, like old earth creationists, to establish their most basic beliefs."[28]

The fact that Scripture, although it could be interpreted in terms of a young earth, does not require such an interpretation. There are other possible interpretations in terms of an ancient earth that do not compromise the authority of Scripture.

The fact that we do not know everything. Humility is often seen in the greatest scientists. It is also a Christian virtue.

Factors essentially the same as the first three of these (with 'young-earth' replaced by 'fixed-earth') would have weighed increasingly with people in the years after Copernicus and Galileo, and would have made them increasingly confident in affirming the new interpretation that fitted more closely with the increased understanding of the universe. There is no reason why the same thing cannot happen today. Just as it was no shame or compromise in the past for people to change their minds over the motion of the earth, so it is no shame or compromise today for people to change their minds about the age of the earth. After all, it was only recently that scientists were persuaded that there was a beginning! That is a good point to recall the fourth factor listed above — the need for humility.

A NECESSARY POSTSCRIPT

I do not wish to leave the matter just here. If I do, readers may think that the only reason for looking at Genesis 1 is to try to settle the matter of its relationship to science. That would be a pity, because it has many other important things to say, as we shall now explain in our final chapter.

NOTES

1. Peter Singer, "Sanctity of Life or Quality of Life?" *Pediatrics* 72, no.1 (July 1983): 128–29.

2. John Gray, *Straw Dogs* (London: Granta Books, 2003), 37.

3. For more on these matters, I refer the reader once more to Lennox, *God's Undertaker*.

4. See the next section below.

5. For comments on genealogies in the Bible and the antiquity of humans, see below.

6. As distinct from the detail of what precisely was involved in the creation of woman, but note that Paul explicitly says that "Adam was formed first, then Eve" (1 Tim. 2:13), and "woman [was made] from man" (1 Cor. 11:8).

7. Denis Alexander, *Creation or Evolution: Do We Have to Choose?* (Oxford: Monarch, 2008), 236ff.

8. Ibid., 237.

9. Ibid., 237–38.

10. Genesis 17:1; 18:1.

11. Alexander, *Creation or Evolution*, 238.

12. Ibid., 193.

13. Alexander, *Creation or Evolution*, 237; emphasis added.

14. See, e.g., Alexander, *Creation or Evolution*, 232.

15. In connection with the obvious fact that there are variations in human beings, it is noteworthy that Paul informs the philosophers at Athens that God made all nations from one man (Acts 17:26).

16. Science cannot rule out this kind of miracle, despite the attempts by thinkers from David Hume to the New Atheists to convince us to the contrary. See Lennox, *God's Undertaker*, chap. 12.

17. K. A. Kitchen, *On the Reliability of the Old Testament* (Grand Rapids: Eerdmans, 2003), 440.

18. Ibid., 441.

19. Nowhere is an apple mentioned.

20. See also John Walton, *The Lost World of Genesis One* (Downers Grove, IL: InterVarsity, 2009), 100.

21. Derek Kidner points out that the assigning of plants for food (1:29–30) to all creatures "must not be pressed to mean that all were once herbivorous, any more than to mean that all plants were

equally edible to all. It is a generalisation that, directly or indirectly, all life depends on vegetation, and the concern of the verse is to show that all are fed from God's hand" (*Genesis* [Leicester, UK: Tyndale Press, 1967], 52).

22. Attributed to the 14th-century English Franciscan thinker William of Ockham, this is the general principle that one should favour a hypothesis that makes the fewest new assumptions among competing hypotheses that are equal in other respects. It does not (falsely) assert that the simplest explanation is always likely to be the correct one.

23. We might add to that a detail concerning the animal sacrifices that were used in Old Testament times to teach Israel the connection between sin and death, and thereby to point forward to the death of Christ as a sacrifice for sins. In the instructions on how to perform the sacrifices it is strongly emphasised that the sacrificial animals should not be diseased. Disease was, in that sense, to be distinguished from death. See Lev. 1:3, 10; 3:1, 6, and many other references.

24. There is endless argument about how we are to understand the tree—literally or metaphorically. In light of our earlier discussion, if we take the tree as metaphorical, we shall immediately be asked the question, a metaphor for what reality? Could it just be that the ancient legends about an elixir of life have a factual basis—that there once was an actual tree of life? In any case we are not (contrary to popular thought) told what the fruit was, so that the important thing is what was represented by it.

25. It is interesting to note that the instruction about vegetation as food for animals (Gen. 1:30) was given to the humans, and not to the animals. Why? One possibility might be as follows. The humans had just been told what their food was to be. They had been commanded to subdue the fish, animals, and birds. It would be important for them to know that that subduing did not include keeping the animals away from the humans' food, suggesting that at least some of them may have had nonvegetarian food. In Genesis 9 there is no explicit commandment to the animals to be carnivorous from now on. But humans are allowed from then on to kill and eat animals.

26. C. S. Lewis, *The Problem of Pain* (New York: Simon & Schuster, 1996), 119.
27. Ibid., 122–23.
28. Paul Nelson and John Mark Reynolds, "Young Earth Creationism," in J. P. Moreland and John Mark Reynolds, eds., *Three Views on Creation and Evolution* (Grand Rapids: Zondervan, 1999), 51.

CHAPTER FIVE

THE MESSAGE OF GENESIS 1

THE BOOK OF GENESIS is foundational for the rest of the Bible. Its opening chapter does something of incalculable importance: it lays down the basis of a biblical worldview.[1] It gives to us humans a metanarrative, a big story into which our lives can be fitted and from which they can derive meaning, purpose, and value. This chapter is devoted to that big story.

GOD EXISTS

One of the most basic big questions we can ask is, what is the nature of ultimate reality? The central tenet of the biblical worldview is that the ultimate reality is God: "In the beginning God ..." Genesis is here making a profound truth-claim: that there is a God. The claim is first stated without any supporting evidence — a circumstance that should not mislead us into deducing that the author of Genesis had no evidence. Both Genesis and the rest of the Bible will subsequently offer that evidence. However, the very manner in which Genesis begins reminds us that every worldview must start somewhere. The Biblical worldview begins with God; the atheist worldview begins with the universe.

However, Genesis 1 does not only tell us that there is a God; it tells us a great deal about him.

GOD IS THE ETERNAL CREATOR

"In the beginning God created the heavens and the earth." Genesis 1:1 thus majestically announces the fact of creation. This is not only a truth claim about God; it is a truth claim about the physical universe. Although the text does not explicitly say that the universe was created from nothing (sometimes expressed by the Latin phrase *ex nihilo*), there are strong arguments for understanding it this way, as many scholars do. Firstly, the phrase "the heavens and the earth" is most likely to be a merism[2] denoting "everything in the material universe," in which case the implication of Genesis 1:1 is ex nihilo creation. There is strong support for this view from the New Testament. Hebrews 11:3: "By faith we understand that the universe was created by the word of God, so that what is seen was not made out of things that are visible." Material is "seen" and "visible," so here is confirmation that, at least, the universe was not made out of preexisting, visible material.[3]

Furthermore, in possibly the clearest New Testament statement of all on the topic, Revelation 4:11 says, "Worthy are you, our Lord and God, to receive glory and honour and power, for you created all things, and by your will they existed and were created." The implication is that the universe came to exist because God created it at some point, so that we may deduce that it was created from nothing, since there was nothing in existence from which to create it — however hard it is for us to get our minds around the idea. All of these later statements have clear roots in Genesis 1:1.

The assertion that God created the physical universe is of paramount importance. It answers the question, why is there something rather than nothing? It implies that this universe cannot explain itself, as secular atheism, by definition, must maintain. It tells us that this material universe is not the ultimate reality. God is.

It is important, of course, not to confuse the fact of creation with the manner or the timing of creation. I mention this because it sometimes happens that failure to sort out problems connected with the manner and timing of creation stops people believing in the fact that creation occurred. An illustration from science can help us grasp the issue here. Stephen Hawking says that space-time began in a singularity, where the laws of physics break down. The moment of creation, therefore, poses an immense problem for science. But this does not stop most scientists believing that there was a beginning. The important thing for these scientists is that there is scientific evidence for a beginning, even though science cannot comprehend the nature of that beginning.[4] We should bear this attitude in mind when we come to Genesis.

Genesis 1:1 anticipates the fuller revelation given to us by John at the beginning of his Gospel in the New Testament: "In the beginning was the Word, and the Word was with God, and the Word was God. He was in the beginning with God. All things were made through him, and without him was not any thing made that was made" (John 1:1 – 3). The word translated "made" means "came to be." God is eternal and uncreated; he did not come to be; he always was. The universe, on the other hand, did "come to be." It was not always there — another strong confirmation, by the way, of ex nihilo creation.

The Genesis account, though not written as polemic, is therefore diametrically opposed to all idolatrous interpretations of the universe, whether of the ancient, pagan kind or the modern secular variety. Genesis clashes head-on with the Babylonian, Canaanite, and Egyptian polytheisms just as much as the Gospel of John contradicts their Greek and Roman equivalents. In particular, ancient Near Eastern accounts typically contain theogonies,[5] which describe how the gods are generated from primeval matter. These gods are, therefore, mere deifications of nature and its powers. This means that such ancient worldviews stand much closer to contemporary materialism than might at first appear. There are contemporary physicists, like Paul Davies for example, who argue that the fine-tuning of the universe indicates that there is great intelligence somewhere; but they hold nevertheless that this intelligence must have evolved from primitive matter: it is, in that sense, of material origin.

One of Richard Dawkins's main *God Delusion* arguments is that, if God created everything, we would have to ask who created God. But the very asking of this question reveals at once that Dawkins has in mind a created God: "Who *created* God?" Created gods certainly are a delusion.

However, the God who is revealed in Genesis is uncreated, so that the "who created God argument" falls to the ground. Dawkins's difficulty must be that he cannot believe in something eternal. Why not? Science certainly does not tell us that there is nothing eternal — indeed, the notion of an eternal universe or eternal energy has dominated human thought for centuries, and still has not disappeared from academic circles.

Furthermore, if Dawkins's question is valid, it can be turned back on him. He believes that the universe created him. Therefore, we are justified in asking him: who created your creator?

The point here is that *all* such questionings must stop with what the questioner believes to be ultimate reality. As we have seen, for the atheist the ultimate reality is the universe, and for the theist the ultimate reality is God. Genesis tells us that God is primary, and the universe derivative. This worldview is the exact opposite of ancient polytheism and contemporary secularism, both of which assume that matter is primary and everything else, including mind, is derivative.

GOD IS DISTINCT FROM HIS CREATION

Furthermore, according to Genesis, God created the universe, but he is not identical with it. Noticeably the sun, moon, and stars are described purely physically, as "lights." There is no hint of conferring any kind of divinity on them as in the contemporary pagan mythologies. Nor is the universe some kind of emanation out of God, like sun rays emanate from the sun. Matter is made out of nothing, not out of God. The Genesis account, therefore, bears no traces of pantheism.

Nor is God the remote deistic "god of the scientists," who started the universe and then retired from the scene, taking no further interest in it. Indeed, the main bulk of the Genesis narrative is devoted to relationships between human beings and God — and, of course, relationships among human beings themselves.

The very fact that such relationships are possible has to do with another profound characteristic of God revealed in Genesis 1.

GOD IS PERSONAL

The phrases "God said," "God saw that it was good," "God blessed," and, above all, "God made man in his own image, male and female he made them" are clear indications that God is a person and not a force. There are dangers in a "Star Wars" mentality that conceives of God as "the Force," for we are persons, and therefore assume, correctly, that we are superior to forces. We harness and use forces; so if we conceive of God as a force, we might wrongly imagine that God is some power that we can harness and use, rather than regarding him as our Creator and Lord, who is worthy of and due our allegiance and worship. It is for him to use us, not for us to use him.

GOD IS A FELLOWSHIP

Genesis 1 talks about the Spirit of God "hovering over the waters" (v. 2) and records God as saying, "Let *us* make man in *our* image" (Gen. 1:26; emphasis added). No explanation is given at this point, but these statements surely anticipate New Testament teaching on the Trinity.[6] This impression is heightened by the repeated use of the phrase: "And God said ..." Creation involves the word of God. Concentrating on that fact, the apostle John begins his Gospel with the magnificent statement, "In the beginning was the Word, and the Word was with God, and the Word was God. He was in the beginning with God. All things were made through Him" (John 1:1 – 3a).

John swiftly identifies the Word with Jesus Christ: "The Word became flesh and dwelt among us, and we have seen his glory, glory as of the only Son from the Father, full of grace and truth" (John 1:14). Thus, God is revealed to us as a tri-unity, a fellowship of Father, Son, and Holy Spirit.

The Apostle Paul says of Christ, "He is the image of the invisible God, the firstborn of all creation. For by him all things were created, in heaven and on earth, visible and invisible, whether thrones or dominions or rulers or authorities—all things were created through him and for him. And he is before all things, and in him all things hold together" (Col. 1:15 – 17).

These are staggering claims to make about anyone in any age, let alone in the twenty-first century. They clearly imply that Christ created space-time. It was he who conceived and, with unimaginable energy and power, spoke into being a material universe, governed by intricate laws that he himself designed. It was his mind that was the mind of God that thought into existence the blueprint for matter, life, and consciousness. Nothing makes sense about Jesus Christ unless he is precisely who he claimed to be—the

Word of God incarnate. Science, as has often been said, cannot rule God out. Jesus Christ has ruled him in.

GOD HAS A GOAL IN CREATION

We noted earlier that the primary impression given by the biblical creation account is that God did not do everything at once. This striking fact immediately raises in our minds the question, what is the goal of the sequence of days? What are they leading up to? The narrative starts with, "In the beginning God created the heavens and the earth." Then we are told that the earth was "without form and void," and God starts to speak. The repeated phrase "And God said ..." marks a sequence of creative and organisational steps by which God shapes the world and fills it with living creatures. In the final step God creates human beings in his image. They represent the pinnacle of God's creation: they alone are said to bear his image. Planet Earth is special. It was created with an ultimate purpose—that of having human beings on it.[7]

The Genesis narrative, therefore, is not just informing us how the universe came to exist. It is also saying why it came to exist. For this reason Genesis emphasises not only the processes of creation, but also God's organisation of the universe in general and the earth in particular, so that it could function as a suitable home for men and women made in his image. Planet Earth has to be given a certain form—light separated from darkness, dry land from sea, visible lights in the sky, plant life to eat—in order for human life to thrive and function as God intended.

This biblical teaching, that the earth was specifically designed as a home for human beings, fits well with what contemporary science tells us about the fine-tuning of the universe. In recent years physicists and cosmologists have discovered that the fundamental constants of nature—those special numbers on which everything depends—have to be "just right" in order for life as we know it to be possible.[8] The Nobel Prize–winning physicist Arno Penzias comments on these remarkable findings: "Astronomy leads us to a unique event, a universe which was created out of nothing, one with the very delicate balance needed to provide exactly the right conditions required to permit life, and one which has an underlying, one might say 'supernatural,' plan."[9] Paul Davies's testimony is again helpful: "I cannot believe that our existence in this universe is a mere quirk of fate, an accident of history, an incidental blip in the great cosmic drama. Our involvement is too intimate.... We are truly meant to be here."[10]

So, both Genesis and science say that the universe is geared to supporting human life. But Genesis says more. It says that you, as a human being, bear the image of God. The starry heavens show the glory of God, yes; but they are not made in God's image. You are. That makes you unique. It gives you incalculable value. The galaxies are unimaginably large compared with you. However, you know that they exist, but they don't know that you exist. You are more significant, therefore, than a galaxy. Size is not necessarily a reliable measure of value, as any woman can tell you as she looks at the diamonds on her finger, and compares them with lumps of coal.

GOD CREATES BY HIS WORD

We have already seen that the fact that God did not do everything at once leads us to think that the purpose of

God's creation of the earth was to be a home for the only beings that bear his image—humans. The individual steps to reach that goal were initiated by God speaking: "And God said ..." This repeated reference to the activity of the word of God in creation resonates very powerfully with me as a scientist. The idea that the universe did not come to be without the input of information and energy from an intelligent source seems to me to have been amply confirmed by scientific discovery.

Firstly, the language of mathematics has proved to be a powerful tool in describing how things work. Its codifications of the laws of nature into short and elegant "words" consisting of symbols surely reflect the greater Word that is ultimately responsible for the physical structures of the universe.

Above and beyond that, there is the major scientific discovery—one of the greatest of all time—that in each of the ten trillion cells of our body we humans possess a "word" of mind-boggling length, the human genome. This "word" is 3.5 billion "letters" long, written in the four chemical "letters" C,G,A,T. Francis Crick and James Watson's Nobel Prize-winning discovery of the double-helix structure of the DNA that carries this genetic information has given rise to the molecular biology revolution—the study of large, information-bearing macromolecules like DNA.

In recent years information has come to be regarded as one of the fundamental concepts of science. One of the most intriguing things about it is that it is not physical. The information you are reading at the moment is carried on the physical medium of paper and ink (or on a physical computer screen). But the information itself is not material.

As I argue in detail elsewhere,[11] the nonmateriality of information points to a nonmaterial source—a mind, the mind of God.

On top of all that, we human beings have also been gifted with a phenomenal facility to use words to describe our universe and to communicate with each other. Does this capacity not point unmistakeably to the vastly greater Word, who has endowed us with his image and imprint? Yet many people write off the claim that Christ is the Word of God as preposterous, and impossible to accept in a scientifically literate age. As a scientist I must confess that I find their attitude very strange. After giving a lecture on "Science and God" to a large group of scientists at a major research establishment, I was (pleasantly) accosted by a physicist, who said, "I deduce from your lecture that you not only believe in God, but you are a Christian. You are therefore obliged to believe that Jesus Christ was simultaneously God and human. How can you, as a scientist, explain that?"

My reaction was to ask him a question as a quid pro quo. And, as I regarded it as a simpler question, I suggested he answer first. "Agreed," he said. "What is consciousness?" I asked. "We don't really know," he responded. "Never mind," I said, "let's try something even simpler. What is energy?" "Well," he replied, "we have equations governing it, we can measure it and use it ..." "That wasn't my question! What *is* energy?" After some thought, he said (as I knew he would), "We don't really know." I then said, "Do you believe in consciousness and in energy?" "Yes," he said. "So you believe in them, and you do not know what they are? Should I write you off as a physicist?" "Please don't," he asked. I responded, "Yet you were prepared to write me off as a scientist, unless

I could explain something vastly more complex than consciousness or energy — the nature of God himself."

"Tell me," I went on: "Why do you believe in consciousness and energy even though you don't understand what they are?" "Well, I suppose it is because these concepts make sense. They have a kind of explanatory power, and you don't have to understand them completely in order to use them to explain other things."

"Precisely," I agreed. "And that is why I believe that Jesus was both man and God. I cannot explain it — by definition it must be one of the most difficult things of any to explain, far more difficult than consciousness or energy — but I believe it because it makes sense of everything else. It is the only interpretation that adequately accounts for Jesus' birth, life, death, resurrection, and ascension."[12]

GOD IS THE SOURCE OF LIGHT

The sequence of days begins with, "And God said, 'Let there be light.'" In a famous passage, Paul draws an analogy between this statement and the proclamation of the Christian message: "For what we proclaim is not ourselves, but Jesus Christ as Lord, with ourselves as your servants for Jesus' sake. For God, who said, 'Let light shine out of darkness,' has shone in our hearts to give the light of the knowledge of the glory of God in the face of Jesus Christ" (2 Cor. 4:5 – 6).

Paul uses creation as a metaphor for what happens to a person at conversion. Once more it is worth stressing that the metaphor denotes something real at a deeper level than the merely physical. The light that God shines into the human heart that trusts him is not physical, of course, but it is real. It is not a matter of mere psychological wishful thinking. The gospel effects an actual spiritual transformation, as Paul goes on to say in the very next chapter, again using the language of creation: "If anyone is in Christ, he is a new creation. The old has passed away; behold, the new has come" (2 Cor. 5:17). It is for this reason that we can have confidence in the Christian message — it brings real illumination, authenticating itself in human experience. It also authenticates itself intellectually, as C. S. Lewis pointed out: "I believe in Christianity as I believe that the sun has risen: not only because I see it, but because by it I see everything else."

But the New Testament has much more to say about this matter of creation light. In fact, Jesus himself refers to the very first occurrence of the word "day" in Genesis and draws from it a surprising and powerful application to our lives. John relates this application in his Gospel as one of the major signs that Jesus performed to confirm his claim to be the Son of God, the Word of God incarnate. It is the famous story of the raising of Lazarus (John 11:1 – 12:11). Lazarus lived with his sisters Mary and Martha in the village of Bethany, near Jerusalem. Lazarus fell ill and the sisters sent a message to Jesus, who had become a friend of the family. Jesus did not respond at once, but remained for two days where he was with his disciples. He then announced to them that he intended to go back to Judaea, as Lazarus was sick. Later Jesus explained to them that he was going in order to awaken Lazarus from the "sleep" of death.

The disciples reacted to Jesus' announcement very negatively: "Rabbi, the Jews were just now seeking to stone you, and are you going there again?" (John 11:8). To the disciples, a trip back to Judaea at that time seemed suicidal. In Galilee, far from Jerusalem, they felt safe; but such was the antagonism that had arisen against Jesus that they were afraid of what might happen if they appeared in or near the capital.

Jesus answered them by referring to the construction of what we call the solar system: "Are there not twelve hours in the day? If anyone walks in the day, he does not stumble, because he sees the light of this world. But if anyone walks in the night, he stumbles, because *the light is not in him*" (John 11:9–10; emphasis added). Jesus was concerned to teach his disciples an important lesson from the very arrangement of the lighting system for our world, as first described in Genesis 1. The lesson is based on the first mention of the word "day": "God called the light Day, and the darkness he called Night" (Gen. 1:5). One could easily miss the fact that it is God who gives the name "day" to the light. Genesis is a book in which God tells humans to get on with the job of naming things, so why does God reserve to himself the giving of names to just a few, a very few, aspects of the created universe? It certainly has the effect of drawing them to our attention, for day and light are not quite the same thing, are they?

Jesus here explains something very important that is easy to miss — the organisation of the world, as distinct from its creation.[13] God's calling of the light "day" and the darkness "night" are not creative acts, in the strict sense. They are organisational. What enables the linguistic distinction to be made is nothing less than the geometrical arrangement of the solar system.

In order to achieve this arrangement, firstly, the source of light for our planet, the sun, has to be physically situated outside our planet home. As Jesus says, the light is not in us. Secondly, earth has to rotate on its own axis, constantly presenting a different face to the sun, so that each earth rotation is divided up into hours of daylight and hours of night. In that sense, day is our experience of the light (of the sun). The light is rationed by the deliberate organisational strategy of the Creator himself.

In order to see why, we need to think once more about day 4. We thought earlier about some of the ways in which people have tried to solve Origen's problem. We found that day 4 is not so concerned about the creation of light (day 1), but about what the sun, moon, and stars, as visible entities in the heavens, were for. The Genesis text tells us explicitly: "Let them be for signs and for seasons, and for days and years" (Gen. 1:14).

In this technological age, those of us who live in cities easily forget the fundamental role played by the sun, moon, and stars in the organisation of life on earth. But for millennia people were dependent on seeing these "lights" in the sky, not only to determine the cycles of seedtime and harvest — the times to graze their animals on the mountains or in the valleys, vital to the sustenance of life — but also to navigate. Those "lights" help humans find their place and time in space-time. It is, surely, the purpose of the sun, moon, and stars that is being emphasised in day 4, not how and when they came into being.

The conversation between Jesus and his disciples that took place in an obscure country tucked away in a corner of the vast Roman Empire twenty centuries ago now takes on an awe-inspiring dimension. The man who addressed the group of disciples that day was none other than the Creator, the Word through whom all things came to exist. He himself was the architect and creator of the solar system about which he was speaking. It was his divine mind that had conceived of the idea of a vast nuclear furnace rolling through trackless space, warping space-time around it and thus holding earth captive in its orbit and bathed in its light and heat. It was his idea to put the source of light outside the world on which he would later place his supreme creation, men and women made in his image. And here he was, the Creator, standing on his specially designed planet Earth, deigning to explain to a group of his human creatures why he had organised the solar system that way. I think we ought to listen, don't you?

The disciples thought that if they followed Jesus back to Judaea it would be suicidal. They would be safe only if they remained where they were. To them this was a matter of simple logic. The authorities in Jerusalem were out to get Jesus, so the safest place for the disciples, they thought, was at a maximum distance from the capital, far away in the provinces. That idea came from inside their heads, of course. That is, they were relying for their guidance on a source of light inside them. But that is not what they did when it came to walking around the countryside. They would travel in daylight, dependent on the external light of the sun. At night they would stumble and be unable to find the way, since *the light was not in them*. They probably did not know, as we know now, that there are certain marine creatures with a light in them. Bioluminescent fish,[14] for instance, produce light by chemical means, and some of them use their light for navigation. Humans are not made that way. They depend on a source of light that not only is not in them; it is not even in their world.[15] The earth was deliberately built like that, spinning round its star 150,000,000 km away, a star on which it is utterly dependent for its light, heat, and energy.

Jesus is, of course, using the arrangement of earth's illumination as a powerful metaphor for something at another level entirely. He expected his disciples to deduce something simple yet profound from his observation about the sun: if in the physical realm they were helplessly dependent on a light situated outside themselves, what about the intellectual, spiritual, and moral realms? Where was the source of their insights and answers, inside or outside their own heads?

This question has lost none of its relevance. The battle between the worldviews of theism and naturalism is about whether or not there is an outside to get guidance from. To the atheist, this universe is a closed system of cause and effect that is ultimately self-explanatory in terms of its basic physics and chemistry, its matter and energy. The only source of wisdom for atheists is from within their own heads.

By contrast, to the biblical theist, this universe is an open system — neither self-existent nor self-explanatory. There is a source of wisdom outside the whole system — God. This means, for instance, that, just as our earth depends on the external sun for its light, so that we cannot even see our planet properly without that light, at the higher level any final explanation of the universe and human beings that does not include God will unravel into darkness. It is for this reason, too, that naturalistic attempts to explain the existence of life solely in terms of the nonliving, of consciousness in terms of the unconscious, of the rational in terms of the nonrational, of human beings solely in terms of animals, of morality in terms of the dictates of pain and pleasure, are bound to fail in the end. The sad irony of the Enlightenment is that it puts the light inside man by making human reason the ultimate arbiter.

So much for the philosophical level. Jesus' words about light and the sun, however, were addressed not to scientists or philosophers but to a group of ordinary men who were fearful about their physical security. The lesson was for them in the first instance. They had perhaps forgotten something that Jesus had already taught them. On a previous visit to Jerusalem he had made another profound statement about light: "I am the light of the world. Whoever follows me will not walk in darkness, but will have the light of life" (John 8:12). That is, Jesus himself is a source of light. Not just any source of light: he is *the* source of light for the world. This is an astonishing statement, parallel to his later claim: "I am ... the truth" (John 14:6). Those of us who are scientists like to think that, somewhere along the line, we have shed at least some little light on a problem, often a very obscure problem, and thus advanced the cause of knowledge in a modest way. A few scientists have had the privilege of shedding light on hitherto intractable human problems, and their solution has brought great benefit — the discovery of penicillin, for instance. But no scientist, in his or her right mind, would ever dream of claiming to be *the* light.

Jesus did — and gave evidence by his life, death, and resurrection that the claim was true.

Furthermore, Jesus implied that he was a *moving* source of light. It is obvious that if a light is moving, it will benefit you only if you keep pace with it. It is the same with Christ. In order to stay in his light and have it illuminate our path, we must keep in step with him: "Whoever follows me will have the light of life."

The challenge to the disciples was clear. The light inside their heads told them they were walking into the dark, probably to their deaths. But Jesus said that if they followed him, a travelling light external to them, they would discover that he was the very light of life. How much of this they understood at the time, we do not know. What we do know is that they followed him; but, by Thomas at least, it was done in a mood of reluctant pessimism: "Let us also go, that we may die with him" (John 11:16). At least they went. And it was good that they did.

The journey led to a graveyard in Bethany, where Lazarus, already four days dead, lay interred in a Middle Eastern tomb, mourned by his sisters. Jesus announced to Martha that her brother Lazarus would rise again. She replied that she fully expected him to rise at the final resurrection at the last day. Upon this, Jesus made a further astounding statement: "I am the resurrection and the life. Whoever believes in me, though he die, yet shall he live, and everyone who lives and believes in me shall never die. Do you believe this?" (John 11:25–26). With remarkable composure she replied, "Yes, Lord; I believe that you are the Christ, the Son of God, who is coming into the world" (John 11:27).

It was not long before her faith was vindicated. Jesus ordered the stone covering the mouth of the tomb to be removed, against realistic protest by Martha that there would be an awful smell. He then commanded Lazarus to come out. And Lazarus, bound with grave-cloths, did just that. It was a spectacular vindication of Christ's claim to be the resurrection and the life. For the disciples it put death into a different light. The Jesus they followed had power over death. They would never think of death in the same way again. And nor should we.

But there was another side. The sisters had sent a message, counting on Jesus' love for the family. They assumed he would come and heal Lazarus. And when he arrived late they remonstrated a little: "Lord, if you had been here, my brother would not have died" (John 11:21, 32). They too had been relying on the light that was in them, and it nearly caused them to doubt the love Jesus had for them. Life's circumstances often do that to us. Sometimes we try to use our powers of reason to make sense of what has happened, and fail. We need light from outside.

There are, of course, no easy answers here, though one thing is clear: atheism has no hope to give. It has no light to shed on death. For atheism, death is the ultimate darkness. But Christ has shown that death is not the end. Furthermore, for those who trust him as Lord and Saviour there is to be a joyful resurrection. The evidence for that is not so much that Jesus raised Lazarus but that he himself rose on the third day and showed himself to many witnesses (1 Cor. 15:1–11).

THE GOODNESS OF CREATION

One cannot read Genesis 1 without noticing the constant refrain, "And God saw that it was good" (Gen. 1:4, 10, 12, 18, 21, 25), culminating in the final assessment on day 6: "And

God saw everything that he had made, and behold, it was very good" (1:31). God is not some distant deistic figure uninterested in his work. He regards his creation with the enthusiasm and joy of a skilful artist who is delighted at what he has done as he sees it formed and organised step by step, until the wonderful harmony of his completed work lies before him, thoroughly fit for the glorious purpose for which he intended it.

Sadly, it would not be long before the original harmony of creation was disrupted, as the first humans failed at the higher level of moral goodness, and sin entered the world to wreak endless havoc. So serious is that moral infection that the business of restoring men and women to fellowship with their Creator will involve something much bigger than creation itself: nothing less than the Creator becoming human, dying at the hands of his creatures and rising again in triumph over sin and death.

Yet at the beginning all was perfect. How different from pantheistic philosophies that regarded matter as essentially evil and held that our wisdom would be to escape from it completely. Indeed, just as the material creation was originally perfect, one day there will be a new creation, new heavens and a new earth that will also be perfect—and righteousness will dwell in them (see 2 Peter 3:13; Rev. 21).

In the meantime, the fact that God has put human beings in charge of a good creation reminds us also of our responsibility towards God as stewards of creation. It is not our property, but God's; and we are not at liberty to abuse, waste, and ruin it. Indeed, God takes our attitude to the earth very seriously, as a day will come in which God will judge those who destroy the earth (Rev. 11:18b).

THE SABBATH

Genesis 1 has much more to teach, but we shall content ourselves by concluding, appropriately enough, with some comments on the Sabbath. Leon Kass reminds us that the Mesopotamians and Babylonians had seven-day cycles that were associated with the phases of the moon; and they had their own *sabattu*, the day of the full moon, which was a day of fasting and ill luck.[16] "In contrast, the seventh day among the children of Israel was completely independent of all ties to the heavens, save to the Creator of the heavens. It established a calendar completely dissociated from the cycles of the heavenly bodies,[17] commemorating instead their Creator, one who stands above and beyond their ceaseless motion."[18] Thus the institution of the Sabbath would remind us of the ever-present danger of human beings becoming subservient to the creation rather than the Creator (Rom. 1:25).

The New Testament mentions the Sabbath in several contexts. We select just one, in which the concept of Sabbath is used to help us grasp a fundamental Christian doctrine that is often misunderstood. The writer to the Hebrews cites the Sabbath passage from Genesis 1 and, after a lengthy discussion of the nature of rest, concludes by saying, "There remains a Sabbath rest for the people of God, for whoever has entered God's rest has also rested from his works as God did from his" (Heb. 4:9–10).

Here, once more, a biblical author uses a concept from Genesis as a metaphor for something real at a deeper level. In this passage, the expression "God's works" refers to the work of creation from which God rested on the seventh day.

God did the creating, and then he rested from it. We inherit a universe that we did not create.

It is important, particularly for those of us who are scientists, to remind ourselves of this fact from time to time. We did not put the universe there. We did not create the objects of scientific study. We study something given. This simple idea has consequences. It means, for instance, that it is for the universe to shape our ideas about how it works, rather than for us to decide in our heads how it ought to work and then force the universe to comply. We all need to be reminded of this and the general principle it enshrines. British Chief Rabbi Jonathan Sacks writes of the Sabbath, "It is a day that sets a limit to our intervention in nature and to our economic activity. We become conscious of being creations, not creators. The earth is not ours, but God's ... The Sabbath is a weekly reminder of the integrity of nature and the boundaries of human striving."[19]

It is those "boundaries of human striving" with which the passage in Hebrews is concerned. All of us long for rest. Not simply the taking of a regular day of rest and recuperation, or going on a much-needed holiday, but respite from the constant pressure to achieve. That pressure turns some people into workaholics, driven by an unreachable goal of the achievement that would give them, they hope, some enduring significance. But there are other things that make us restless—loneliness, broken relationships, frustration, unfulfilled desires, guilt, pain, illness, hurt, burdens of family and friends, and a multitude of other things. We are restless beings. Augustine of Hippo long ago traced the reason for this back to creation: "You have made us for yourself, Lord, and our hearts are restless until they rest in you."[20]

Augustine was surely thinking of the solution to this restlessness that was given by Jesus himself: "Come to me, all who labor and are heavy laden, and I will give you rest. Take my yoke upon you, and learn from me, for I am gentle and lowly in heart, and you will find rest for your souls. For my yoke is easy, and my burden is light" (Matt. 11:28–30).

Jesus' invitation is clear. That rest comes when we are prepared to come to him and accept what he calls "my yoke," that is, accept his authority and leadership. At the heart of Christianity is a willingness to trust Jesus Christ as Lord and Saviour and thereby receive forgiveness and peace with God. The problem is that, in a world where achievement and merit count for so much, we human beings find it difficult to understand and accept that God's forgiveness and peace cannot be earned by our work, effort, or merit, but must be received as a free gift.

And that, says the letter to Hebrews, is where the Sabbath can help us. Not now at the level of resting one day in seven, but in understanding the principle that is involved. God did the work of creating the universe, and then he rested. We inherit a creation that we didn't work for, merit, or earn. In that sense, we rest in what God has done. Entering God's spiritual rest—receiving his forgiveness, salvation, and peace—proceeds in exactly the same way. God has completed the work on which salvation rests: the death of Christ for human sin on the cross. In order to enter God's rest, we must rest on the work that Christ has done—not on the work we do. Paul makes this principle crystal clear: "Now to the one who works, his wages are not counted as a gift but as his due. And to the one who does not work but trusts him who justifies the ungodly, his faith is counted as righteousness" (Rom. 4:4–5).

BACK TO THE BEGINNING: A PERSONAL NOTE

It is now over forty years since I was married. In our wedding service, Sally and I were addressed by an extraordinary man. In his youth he had been a heavyweight boxer of the sort who took on all comers at fairgrounds. When he became a Christian, his life took on a markedly different character. He went back to school as an adult and sat with the children to try to catch up on his education. He had a prodigious memory and was able to develop an encyclopaedic knowledge of the Bible, which he then used to great effect in communicating the Christian faith to everyone from shipyard workers to Cambridge students, all of whom loved him for his directness and honesty. His name was Stan Ford.

His wedding address centred on the text, "In the beginning God created the heavens and the earth." Stan was no scientist, though he respected learning; but the point that he made that day has reverberated powerfully through our married life. It was based on the first four words of his text: "In the beginning God ..." A wedding was a new beginning, he said, and there would be many other new beginnings in the future. The foundation for every new beginning was that God should be in on it. We have proved him right. What would a beginning be without God? The universe itself couldn't have started without him.

If some of this sounds too much like preaching, just remember that we are not critical of people who are passionate about science or football! In any case, I don't think it will do any harm. It is one thing to wrestle with the meaning of the days of Genesis; it is another to understand, apply, and live the whole message of Genesis. And if we are not doing the latter, I am not sure that the former will profit us much.

Come to think of it, I never did ask Stan about the days. Too late now. The irony is that he now knows much more about them than I do, or ever will—in this life.

What, therefore, should our attitude be to others who do not agree with us, whatever view we hold? Surely the old adage has got it more or less right: "In essentials, unity; in nonessentials, liberty; and in all things, charity."

But there we really must let matters rest! It is high time for a Sabbath!

NOTES

1. Furthermore, that worldview best explains why science is possible. See John C. Lennox, *God's Undertaker: Has Science Buried God?* (Oxford: Lion Hudson, 2009), 20ff.

2. That is, a figure of speech in which a totality is expressed by referring to its contrasting parts. Another example of this in Genesis is the phrase "the knowledge of good and evil" which, it is suggested, is a merism for "the knowledge of everything."

3. Interestingly, creation ex nihilo is supported by the Jewish writer of 2 Maccabees: "I beg you, my child, to look at the heaven and the earth and see everything that is in them, and recognize that God did not make them out of things that existed" (7:28–29 NRSV).

4. Note that this analogy applies to the manner, rather than the timing, of creation, since the timing is part of the Standard (Big Bang) Model.

5. See appendix A.

6. Although the word *Trinity* does not appear in the New Testament, Thomas Torrance has pointed out that the doctrine of the

Trinity is not so much a Christian formulation as it is the way that God has revealed himself. See his *The Christian Doctrine of God* (Edinburgh: T&T Clark, 1996).

7. It is therefore fitting that the description of the sixth day is longer than that of the other days.

8. See Lennox, *God's Undertaker*, chap. 4.

9. Arno Penzias, "Creation Is Supported by All the Data So Far," in Henry Margenau and Roy A. Varghese, eds., *Cosmos, Bios, Theos: Scientists Reflect on Science, God, and the Origins of the Universe, Life, and Homo Sapiens* (La Salle, IL: Open Court, 1992), 83.

10. Paul Davies, *The Mind of God* (London: Simon and Schuster, 1992), 232.

11. Lennox, *God's Undertaker*, 177–78.

12. For the related objection that science and miracle are incompatible, see Lennox, *God's Undertaker*, 135–92.

13. This emphasis was first pointed out to me by Professor David W. Gooding.

14. Biologist Andrew Parker, author of *The Genesis Enigma* (London: Doubleday, 2009), is a world authority in this field.

15. If the sun were to be extinguished, human life would not survive for long—even with artificial sources of light and heat.

16. See also Gordon J. Wenham, *Genesis 1–15*, Word Biblical Commentary (Waco, TX: Word Books, 1987), 35, who suggests that the Sabbath may have been introduced as a deliberate counterblast to the Mesopotamian lunar-regulated cycle.

17. It is good to remind ourselves of this since our English names of the days of the week are derived from the names of planets and pagan deities.

18. Leon Kass, *The Beginning of Wisdom* (Chicago: University of Chicago Press, 2006), 52.

19. Jonathan Sacks, *The Dignity of Difference: How to Avoid the Clash of Civilisations* (New York and London: Continuum, 2002), 167.

20. Augustine, *Confessions,* Books 1–4, ed. G. Clark (Cambridge: Cambridge University Press, 2001), 84.

A BRIEF BACKGROUND TO GENESIS

THE BOOK OF GENESIS was originally written in Hebrew, and its title in that language comes from the very first word in the text, *bereš'it*, which means "In the beginning."[1] The title "Genesis" (Greek for "origin") was given to the book by its early Greek translators.

Edward J. Young, a distinguished Hebrew scholar, says that the text has the marks of a prose narrative describing a succession of events. It lacks a major characteristic of Hebrew poetry, namely two-line parallelism, where a statement is made on one line and then repeated in different words on the next line. For example:

> To you, O LORD, I cry,
> And to the Lord I plead for mercy. (Ps. 30:8)

However, Young also points out that Genesis 1 has certain features that would be unusual in straight prose. For example, it contains repeated refrains like "and God saw that it was good," and repetitions like "And God said," "let there be," and "and it was so." Hence the impression given is of a text that is written in "exalted, semipoetical language," in the sense that it features certain semipoetical elements that serve to make it memorable but do not take away from an ordered narrative purpose. Indeed, both phrases mentioned above serve to introduce what are clearly nonpoetic factual statements about the creation and organisation of the physical universe itself.

Regarding the genre of Genesis 1, C. John Collins writes, "We have called the passage a narrative, and this is proper because of the prominent use of the *wayyiqtol*² to denote successive events. But we must acknowledge that it is an unusual narrative indeed: not only because of the unique events described and the lack of other actors besides God, but also because of the highly patterned way of telling it all."[3]

The Genesis text comes to us from the ancient Near East, and so any attempt to understand it will be enriched by knowledge of the literature and culture of the time. But what culture, at what time? Genesis talks about the foundation of the great cities of the ancient Near East in Mesopotamia, and it describes the pilgrimage of Abraham from Ur of the Chaldees to Canaan and the life of his children in Canaan, followed by the movement of his family to Egypt. Thus the cultures of Mesopotamia, Canaan, and Egypt come into the picture. Traditionally, although his name is not mentioned in the book, the authorship of Genesis is ascribed to Moses, and Genesis is often called "The First Book of Moses."[4] This would mean that it dates from somewhere around the fifteenth to thirteenth centuries BC.

As to how the Genesis text was understood by those living in the culture that it ultimately generated, we have the evidence of the Old and New Testaments to show us that they took the Genesis material as history. The Jewish historian Josephus, in his introduction to his famous Jewish Antiquities, written around AD 110, demonstrates an acute awareness of the difference between a carefully researched factual account of history, on the one hand, and fables and deliberate fabrications on the other.

In this regard it is interesting to compare the Genesis account with the literature of contemporary ancient cultures. One important example is the Babylonian epic *Enuma Elish*, whose title means "When on high," translating the first two words of this epic that was written in the Old Babylonian period[5] (second millennium BC) and completed about 1000 BC, according to ancient Near Eastern scholar K. A. Kitchen.[6] *Enuma Elish* was a story of great cultural importance among the Babylonians, and its recitation by the priests formed the centrepiece of the fourth day of the annual New Year Festival. However, *Enuma Elish* is not so much an account of creation as the story of war among the Babylonian gods. It relates how the god Marduk gained his supremacy, with creation as a by-product of his battle. Marduk defeated the goddess Ti'amat and split her body into two pieces. With one piece he made the earth, and with the other the sky. In the Babylonian account, then, creation is secondary; the gods and their wars take centre stage.[7] Here are the first few lines to give the flavour of the epic:

Enuma Elish la nabu shamanu...
When on high the heaven had not been named

Firm ground below had not been called by that name
Naught but primordial Apsu, their begetter.
(And) Mummu (and?) Tiamat, she who bore them all,
Their waters commingling as a single body;
No reed-hut had been matted, no marsh land had
    appeared;
When no gods whatever had been brought into being,
Uncalled by name, their destinies undetermined –
Then it was that the gods were formed within them …[8]

Attention has been drawn to certain similarities between the Genesis account and *Enuma Elish*. For instance, *Enuma Elish* is written on seven tablets, and the Genesis account speaks of seven days; there is a similar order of creation — heavens, sea, and earth; and in the sixth tablet, as on the sixth day, human beings are created.

These correspondences have led some scholars to surmise that the Genesis account is derived from the Babylonian *Enuma Elish* (and, arguing similarly, that the Genesis narrative of the flood derives from the Epics of *Gilgamesh* and *Atrahasis*[9]). They think that the idea of God transforming an initial chaos into a cosmos is a throwback, not simply to an early state of the universe but to myths concerning a primeval chaotic power that was pitted against the gods. Some additionally hold that these dependencies show that Genesis is of comparatively late date, having been composed in the time of the Jewish exile in Babylon in the sixth century BC.[10]

However, many scholars point out that the surface similarities mask much more significant differences. Most striking is the fact that Genesis lacks the central theme of the Babylonian epic, theogony, that is, an account of the genesis of the gods, which is a common characteristic of ancient Near Eastern mythologies.[11] The God of Genesis is utterly distinct. He was not created by the universe, as were the pagan gods. It is the other way round. The God of Genesis is not a created God at all; he is the Creator of the universe.

Furthermore, according to Genesis, human beings are created in the image of God as the pinnacle of His creation: "Let us make man in our own image"; according to the *Enuma Elish*, on the other hand, human beings are created as an afterthought to lighten the work of the gods:

> I will establish a savage (lullu), 'man' shall be his name,
> Verily, savage-man I will create,
> He shall be charged with the service of the gods
> That they might be at ease.[12]

Also, by contrast with the Mesopotamian myths, Genesis has no multiplicity of warring gods and goddesses; the heavens and earth are not made out of a god; there are no mythical beasts; and, strikingly, there are no deifications of stars, planets, sun, and moon — the usual names of the last two are not even used in Genesis 1.

The universe to which Genesis introduces us is no mythical construct; it is our familiar world, with light, sky, sea, and land; sun, moon, and stars; plants, fish, and animals; and human beings. Genesis is concerned with actual and not mythical events in the world. And over it all, God the uncreated Creator presides, speaking his creative Word so that all is accomplished. If Genesis depends on the Babylonian account, as is claimed, why then is it so utterly different from that account? Its assertion that there is only one God, the Creator who is distinct from his creation, stands in direct contradiction to the idolatrous interpretations of the universe that lay at the heart of the polytheistic mythologies of Babylon and elsewhere.[13] By ascribing creation to one supreme God who is not himself part of creation, Genesis protests by its very nature against such polytheism.[14] For instance, ascribing to the sun the humble role of light bearer rather than god would be a powerful challenge to the mythology of the land of Joseph's rule and of Moses' upbringing, where the supreme god was the sun god Ra, whose name was embedded in the title of the ruler Pha-*ra*-oh.

One response to this paradoxical situation is the suggestion that an original mythological text has undergone a process of gradual de-deification—a removal of the mythological gods and ideas in order to turn it into a protest against the idolatry of Babylon that so grieved the Jews in exile.[15] However, K. A. Kitchen disagrees: "The common assumption that the Hebrew account is simply a purged and simplified version of the Babylonian legend (applied also to the flood stories) is fallacious on methodological grounds. In the Ancient Near East, the rule is that simple accounts or traditions may give rise (by accretion and embellishment) to elaborate legends, but not vice versa. In the Ancient Orient, legends were not simplified or turned into pseudo-history (historicized) as has been assumed for early Genesis."[16]

In any case, no de-deification took place, for the simple reason that there was no need for it. The Genesis account was written by someone who never did believe in a multiplicity of gods in the first place.

The idea of the book being a product of substantial revision and reinterpretation of earlier mythologies is also rejected by Alan Millard, who discovered and deciphered one of the ancient Babylonian flood texts that had been left forgotten in a drawer in the British Museum. Millard points out, "It has yet to be shown that there was borrowing, even indirectly ... all who suspect or suggest borrowing by the Hebrews are compelled to admit large-scale revision, alteration, and reinterpretation in a fashion which cannot be substantiated for any other composition from the Ancient Near East or in any other Hebrew writing."[17]

More recently, Kitchen argues that although there are analogies between the contents of Genesis 1–11 and the rich literary heritage from the ancient Near East, in the sense that the Genesis narratives also speak of creation and a flood,[18] there is no direct relationship between Genesis and these other traditions: "Despite the repeated claims of an older generation of biblical scholars, *Enuma Elish* and Genesis 1–2 share no direct relationship. Thus the word *tehom/thm* is common to both Hebrew and Ugaritic (North Syrian), and means nothing more than 'deep, abyss.' It is not a deity, like Ti'amat, a goddess in *Enuma Elish*."[19] Elsewhere he sums up: "The attempts made in the past to establish a definite relationship between Genesis and Babylonian epics such as *Enuma Elish* have now had to be abandoned; in content, aim, theology and philology there is divergence and no proven link."[20]

This brings us back to the matter of dating. Kitchen points out several strands of evidence that converge on an early date:

1. The topic of the division of languages mentioned in Genesis 11 is very old—it is also recorded in a nineteenth-/eighteenth-century Sumerian composition in relation to a king who lived around 2600 BC.
2. The kind of structure exhibited by Genesis 1–11 is not known in the ancient Near East after 1600 BC and is characteristic of documents before that time.
3. The scribal use of cuneiform script spread from Mesopotamia as far as Canaan, Hazor, and even Hebron by the seventeenth century BC, so that the account could have been written as early as that time.

Kitchen sums up the evidence as follows:

> So no objection can be taken to the essence of Genesis 1–11 going westward at this epoch; its written formulation in early Hebrew may then have followed later and independently. The patriarchal tradition would then have been passed down in Egypt (as family tradition) to the fourteenth/thirteenth century, possibly then first put into writing … It is part of the oldest levels of Hebrew tradition, as were the Mesopotamian accounts in their culture.

As to biblical records of creation that do have a later date, Kitchen adds:

> In biblical terms the Genesis 1–11 account stands in sharpest contrast with the only other extensive Hebrew account of origins, which began from the beginning—by that indubitably postexilic writer, the Chronicler, from circa 430 … It is noteworthy that he did not give a later version of creation, fall, and flood, etc., but simply summed up baldly the

entire "history" from Adam to Abraham genealogically in just the first part of a chapter (1 Chronicles 1.1–28). Fashions had changed radically between the nineteenth and the fifth centuries in this regard as well as in so much else in ancient life.[21]

By now the attentive reader may be asking how the date of composition of the original text of Genesis can have any real importance, since the polytheisms of the time of Moses were not, after all, much different from those of the period of the Jewish Babylonian exile. Placing the main emphasis on the polytheistic background (which the text itself does not explicitly mention) can take attention away from the foreground, the matter of origins (which the text does explicitly mention). For instance, it is frequently suggested that the text of Genesis is theological and literary, as distinct from historical or scientific, as if these are the only categories that should be considered, or, perhaps more importantly, as if they are mutually exclusive categories. It is, however, perfectly possible for a text simultaneously to inform us about objective facts and to have a theological purpose. Genesis does precisely that. In the words of C. John Collins: "Genesis is offering us the true story of mankind's past."[22]

NOTES

1. This usage is very ancient and was common in the ancient Semitic world from eighteenth century BC. See K. A. Kitchen, *The Old Testament in Its Context*, www.biblicalstudies.org.uk/pdf/ot_context–1_kitchen.pdf old_testament_in_its_context, pp. 9–10.
2. A Hebrew verbal form.
3. C. John Collins, *Genesis 1–4: A Linguistic, Literary, and Theological Commentary* (Phillipsburg, NJ: P&R, 2006), 43.

4. In German, for example.

5. Georges Roux, *Ancient Iraq* (London: Penguin, 1992), 95.

6. K. A. Kitchen, *On the Reliability of the Old Testament* (Grand Rapids: Eerdmans, 2003), 424.

7. Kitchen writes, "In terms of theme, creation is the massively central concern of Gen. 1–2, but it is a mere tailpiece in *Enuma Elish*, which is dedicated to portraying the supremacy of the god Marduk of Babylon" (Ibid.).

8. Roux, *Ancient Iraq,* 96.

9. Dating from the first half of the second millennium BC. See Kitchen, *On the Reliability of the Old Testament*, 423.

10. Often on the basis of the largely abandoned so-called Documentary Hypothesis that was popular in the first part of the last century.

11. Such theogonies typically describe how the gods are generated from primeval matter so that the gods are, in contemporary terminology, deifications of nature and its powers. These gods were thus "material" gods, which means that such ancient worldviews stand much closer to contemporary materialism than might at first appear.

12. Roux, *Ancient Iraq,* 98.

13. There are major similarities between the polytheisms of Assyria, Egypt, Canaan, and Babylon.

14. Paul protests against the idolatry of the Athenians, using precisely this argument from creation. See Acts 17:22–25.

15. Analogous to the de-deification of the universe that was necessary in Greek thought, in order for scientific thinking to begin.

16. K. A. Kitchen, *Ancient Orient and Old Testament* (London: Tyndale Press, 1966), 89.

17. Alan Millard, "A New Babylonian 'Genesis Story,'" in Richard S. Hess and David T. Tsumura, eds., *I Studied Inscriptions from before the Flood: Ancient Near Eastern and Literary Approaches to Genesis 11* (Winona Lake, IN: Eisenbrauns Inc., 1994).

18. It should be mentioned that parallel traditions are evidence that there was a common event that triggered them. For instance, the famous Sumerian King List gives a list of kings and dynasties before the Flood, then the Flood, and then a long sequence of post-diluvian dynasties. This document dates to the twentieth to nineteenth centu-

ries BC. Kitchen makes the point, "The importance of this document for our purpose is that it shows the Sumero-Babylonian conviction that a specific flood once interrupted the course of their very earliest history and was ipso facto a historical event in their reckoning. Therefore, on that showing the event attested also by Genesis and the epics belongs to 'proto-history,' not to myth." See K. A. Kitchen, *The Old Testament in Its Context*, www.biblicalstudies.org.uk/pdf/ot_context−1_kitchen.pdf old testament in its context, 3.

19. Kitchen, *On the Reliability of the Old Testament*, 424.
20. K. A. Kitchen, *The Old Testament in its Context*, www.biblicalstudies.org.uk/pdf/ot_context−1_kitchen.pdf old testament in its context, 3.
21. Kitchen, *On the Reliability of the Old Testament*, 427.
22. Collins, *Genesis 1−4*, 243.

THE COSMIC TEMPLE VIEW

THE IDEA THAT THE EARLY CHAPTERS of Genesis have to do with the creation of a "cosmic temple" has been advanced in various forms by a number of authors. For instance, Gordon Wenham points out that many of the features of the garden of Eden are also to be found in later sanctuaries, particularly in the tabernacle, or the Jerusalem temple. He regards these parallels as suggesting that "the garden itself is understood as a sort of sanctuary."[1] Rikki E. Watts, who holds the framework view, points out that the Old Testament is "awash with architectural imagery when describing creation" (like the famous foundations and pillars of the earth that we looked at earlier). From this perspective he views Genesis 1 "as a 'poetic' account in which Yahweh, Israel's god, is proclaimed the builder of creation, his palace-temple. It is he who by the fiat of his kingly command provided the fundamental structures of ancient human experience and who filled these sub-realms with their rulers, over all of which he has placed humanity, his image-bearer, as his vice regent."[2]

More recently John Walton writes, "From the idea that the temple was considered a mini-cosmos, it is easy to move to the idea that the cosmos could be viewed as a temple."[3] Now, although Walton is a Hebrew specialist, a third of his book is taken up with the implications of his work for the relationship between science and the Genesis record. That emboldens me, as a scientist who is deeply interested in language and the logic of argument (though not a Hebrew specialist), to make some comment on what Walton has written.

A FUNCTIONAL ONTOLOGY FOR GENESIS 1?

What particularly interests me about Walton's work is not so much that there may be some correspondence between the cosmos and the temple, but his conviction that Genesis 1 does not refer to material creation at all, that it is, rather, a functional account of the cosmos as a temple. Walton believes, of course, that God was involved in the material origins of the universe. His contention is, however, that "Genesis 1 is not that story,"[4] but an account of "functional origins." Walton admits, "Theoretically it could be both. But assuming that we simply must have a material account if we are going to say anything meaningful, is cultural imperialism."[5]

Is it really a question of the cultural imperialism of a prior "must"? The idea that ancient readers universally thought in functional terms sits at odds with Walton's own assertion, that his view is "not a view that has been rejected by other scholars; it is simply one they have never considered because their material ontology was a blind presupposition for which no alternative was ever considered."[6] This is a very surprising statement. Surely, if ancient readers thought only in functional terms, the literature would be full of it, and scholars would be very aware of it?

One of the central planks of Walton's argument is that the ontology of Genesis 1 is functional and not material. He claims that "people in the ancient world believed that something existed not by virtue of its material properties, but by virtue of its having a function in an ordered system. Here I do not refer to an ordered system in scientific terms, but an ordered system in human terms, that is in relation to society and culture."[7]

Walton claims that there is evidence for this view from ancient Near Eastern accounts. However, since the biblical account differs significantly from those accounts, as appendix A shows, it is hard to see just what weight to attach to this argument. In any case, Walton lays great stress on the meaning of the Hebrew word *bara* ("create") and claims that it concerns functions. He lists some words that form objects of *bara* and claims that the "grammatical objects of the verb are not easily identifiable in material terms,"[8] although he offers no detailed analysis. Looking at his list, however, I form the impression that many of the objects of *bara* are easily identifiable in material terms, especially those that occur in Genesis.

Genesis 1:1 refers to the creation of the heaven and earth. There is no hint here of a functional dimension "in relation to society and culture" — humans have not yet been created. Similarly Genesis 1:21 speaks of the creation of the great sea creatures. Here again there is no functional dimension. Genesis 1:27 refers to the creation of human beings in his image as male and female. Here there is surely both a physical dimension and a functional dimension, the latter being emphasized in the subsequent command to be fruitful and multiply and fill the earth and subdue it. Indeed, I was encouraged to read that Walton posited substantive discontinuity between evolutionary processes and the creation of the historical Adam and Eve.[9] Genesis 2:3 refers to God resting from "all his work that he had done in creation," thus including both bringing the world, creatures, and humans into existence and giving them functions. Genesis 2:4 refers again to "the day that the LORD God made the earth and the heavens," without a hint of function. Genesis 5:1 says, "This is the book of the generations of Adam. When God created man, he made him in the likeness of God." The context is that of Adam and his physical descendants, leading into a discussion of the problems occasioned by the constitution of human beings as part spirit and part flesh, rather than function. The final reference in Genesis is 6:7, where God says: "I will blot out man whom I have created"—a clear reference to physical death caused by a very material flood.[10]

The linguistic evidence cited by Walton seems, therefore, to undermine his case, rather than support it.

Walton then argues that his thesis is supported by the fact that in contexts where *bara* is used, no materials are ever mentioned. He points out that many scholars—surely not unreasonably—have deduced from this that creation ex nihilo is intended. He then says that such a conclusion "assumes that 'create' is a material activity." He continues, "If, as the analysis of objects presented above suggests, *bara* is a functional activity, it would be ludicrous[11] to expect that materials are being used in the activity."[12]

The logic here seems faulty. Firstly, as we have just said, the analysis of grammatical objects does not appear to support Walton's thesis. Secondly, the absence of materials in connection with *bara* is surely to be taken in conjunction with the repeated, and therefore emphatic, presence of the phrase indicative of what was involved in the acts of creation: "And God said." In the New Testament we find the highly illuminating statement, "By faith we understand that the universe was created by the word of God, so that what is seen was not made out of things that are visible" (Heb. 11:3). This text occurs in a chapter that is thoroughly steeped in the language of Genesis; indeed Hebrews 11 can be seen as a key New Testament exposition of Genesis, beginning with creation.

The point that is being made in Genesis 1, as we have previously indicated, is that the universe was indeed made ex nihilo by the word of God, which is invisible, indeed immaterial. This looks like powerful biblical evidence that the contextual conjunction of *bara* with God speaking in Genesis 1 indicates that Genesis 1 has very much to do with material origins — the origin of matter itself.[13]

Furthermore, the major New Testament account of creation at the beginning of the Gospel of John has an important material aspect to it. John writes of the Word of God, "All things were made through him, and without him was not any thing made that was made" (John 1:3). Earlier we pointed out that the Greek word here translated "made" means "came to be." It therefore refers to material existence. John contrasts God the Word, who is eternal and never came to be, with the material universe ("all things"), which is not eternal: it did come to be. Thus Walton's conclusions are not valid for the biblical doctrine of creation as a whole.

THE COSMIC TEMPLE METAPHOR

Although my concern is principally with Walton's "functional" interpretation of Genesis 1, reading the "cosmic temple" aspect of his work also raises a number of issues in my mind.

Attention has been drawn to a correspondence between the summary comments on the creation sequence in Genesis 1:31 – 2:3 and the concluding remarks on the completion of the tabernacle in Exodus 39. Robert Gordon writes that this can be explained satisfactorily by the depiction of God as workman in Genesis 1 – 2. He continues, "One explanation of this correspondence is that creation is viewed as a sanctuary in Genesis 1 – 2: God is making a cosmos fit for his presence just as the tents and temples of the historical period were constructed as his dwelling-places on earth." He cautions, "Such a reading of creation in Genesis may work better in chapters 2 – 3, where there are elements redolent of the sanctuary traditions of the Old Testament ... but less obviously in chapter 1. More probably the creation-tabernacle correspondence arises because creation is being treated as a building."[14]

Yet Walton writes, "Without hesitation the ancient reader would conclude that this is a temple text and that day seven is the most important of the seven days. In a material account seven would have little role, but in a functional account ... it is the true climax without which nothing else would make any sense or have any meaning."[15]

The assertion that an ancient reader would "without hesitation ... conclude" that this was a functional account of creation written as a temple text is a very sweeping statement, in view of the following. No sources are cited to demonstrate that this is what ancient readers would instinctively have thought. Furthermore, which ancient readers are we talking about? The word *temple* occurs nowhere in the text, which is not surprising in light of the dating of the text given in appendix A.[16] The text that Walton cites as his clearest evidence that the cosmos was to be thought of as a temple comes from much later in Israel's history. It is Isaiah 66:1 – 2:

> Thus says the LORD:
> "Heaven is my throne,
> and the earth is my footstool;
> what is the house that you would build for me,
> and what is the place of my rest?
> All these things my hand has made,
> and so all these things came to be,"
> declares the Lord.

Walton also cites Solomon's prayer at the temple dedication: "But will God indeed dwell on the earth? Behold, heaven and the highest heaven *cannot* contain you; how much less this house that I have built!" (1 Kings 8:27; emphasis added).[17]

Granted that the idea of the cosmos as a temple had been around in the ancient Near East, far from seeing the heavens as a temple where God dwelt, Solomon's perception appears to have led him in the exact opposite direction — that the heavens cannot contain the Almighty. Is Isaiah really expecting us to draw a temple analogy with the cosmos, or is he, like Solomon, pointing out that the cosmos is still too small to contain God?

Whatever the answer to this question, what strikes me about the whole discussion is that Walton's exclusion of the material dimension now seems even more arbitrary, since the parallel texts he cites give great prominence to the *material* construction of the tabernacle and temple and the articles of furniture associated with them — and not only to their function. This, as C. John Collins points out, undermines Walton's thesis that Genesis 1 is not concerned with materials.[18]

Furthermore, the key text cited by Walton above (Isaiah 66:1–2) refers explicitly to the fact of the making of the heaven and the earth by "[God's] hand," with the result, not that they received a function, but that they came into existence.[19]

Finally, it is perhaps worth pointing out that the climax of Genesis 1 would appear to be, not God taking up residence in a cosmic temple, but human beings, created in the image of God, taking up residence as God's vice-regents on earth.

THE SIGNIFICANCE OF THE SEVENTH DAY

Yet Walton claims, "The most central truth to the creation account is that this world is a place for God's presence ...

The establishment of the functional cosmic temple is effectuated by God taking up his residence on day seven." However, there is not the slightest hint in the text of God so doing, let alone this being "the most central truth." Walton also suggests (following Moshe Weinfeld) that Genesis 1 might have been "a recounting of the functional origins of the cosmos as a temple that was rehearsed yearly to celebrate God's creation and enthronement in the temple," though he admits that any definitive evidence of such a festival is lacking.[20]

A puzzling feature of Walton's work is that he does not appear to tell us in the end what the days of Genesis 1 actually represent.[21] He says that they are twenty-four-hour days of one week,[22] but which week is being referred to and what exactly happened in it are not at all clear from his description. He suggests, in light of the ubiquity of the number seven in connection with temple accounts, that the days "may be understood in relation to some aspect of temple inauguration," arguing that "the temple is created in the inauguration ceremony. So also the cosmic temple would be made functional (created) in an inauguration ceremony."[23] But what does this mean? Also, what does it actually mean for God to take up residence in this temple?

Interestingly enough, we do have detailed examples in the Old Testament of God taking up his residence in the tabernacle and in the temple of Solomon. Is it not strange, therefore, that Scripture mentions these in considerable detail, and yet has nothing explicit to say about a major ceremony that, if Walton is right, has foundational cosmic significance and was regularly celebrated as such?

However, to set against Walton's conjectures, there is clear evidence in Scripture of a weekly celebration of day seven that was part of the law of God as given to Israel — the Sabbath rest. And we are told that it is the cessation of work that is emphasized in the weekly celebration of the Sabbath that is enjoined in the law (Exod. 20:8 – 11). The Sabbath had a very material emphasis for Israel, therefore, so that it is very hard to imagine that they thought the record of God's work in Genesis 1 had no such emphasis, as Walton suggests.

Furthermore, the fact that the Sabbath rest of God marked an end to the period of creating and organizing the universe makes an important theological point about the physical universe that has profound scientific implications. That is, God's creation of the universe is *not* the same as his upholding of the universe, so that the past cannot be exhaustively explained in terms of physical processes going on in the present.[24]

THE SCIENTIFIC PERSPECTIVE

It is surely fair to say that most people throughout the ages have understood Genesis 1:1 to be referring to the creation of the physical universe, and therefore making a cosmological statement that is understandable to all ages and cultures. However, Walton suggests that this reaction to the text is evidence that we are failing to look at it through the eyes of those to whom it was originally addressed. He argues that Genesis 1 is ancient cosmology, in the sense that "it does not attempt to address cosmology in modern terms or address modern questions. The Israelites received no revelation to update or modify their 'scientific' understanding of the cosmos."[25] Walton holds that one of the main problems in the current debate is making what he calls the "concordist" mistake of seeking to give contemporary scientific explanations for the text, and therefore pressing the text to say things that it never intended.

Walton is surely right to warn us of the danger of ignoring context and forcing the text to say more than the author intended it to say. However, I wonder also if there is an equal and opposite danger of forcing the text to say less than the author intended it to say. While agreeing that Genesis 1 does not "attempt to address modern cosmology in modern terms," I am also not convinced that it altogether fails to address questions that have cosmological content. For instance, the question whether the universe has a beginning or not has been around for millennia, but it continues to be a very modern question, with the breakthrough (from the scientific perspective) occurring as recently as the 1960s, even though the Bible has always stated in unequivocal language that there was a beginning.[26]

Secondly, is it really true that the Israelites "received no revelation to update or modify their 'scientific' understanding of the cosmos"?[27] Granted, we are not speaking here of "science" in the sense of modern cosmology or mathematical physics, but rather in terms of true understanding of aspects of the physical universe. At this level, it is reasonable to ask what "scientific understanding of the cosmos" did the Hebrews have, and where did they get it? As Walton explicitly refers to Israelites, presumably their main understanding of the cosmos came from Genesis, which was not simply an "updating" of the prevalent cosmologies of the ancient

Near East: it was uniquely distinct from those cosmologies, as Walton himself admits. In contrast to the view that the universe was made from preexisting gods, Genesis teaches that the universe was created by one God who spoke it into existence from nothing.[28]

What is even more telling, for me as a mathematician, is that Genesis 1 separates God's creation and organization of the universe into six days, each of which begins with the phrase "And God said ..." Now, doubtless this is language that predates modern scientific language, by definition. It would, however, be rather unwise to dismiss it as having nothing significant to say. For the very same emphasis on God speaking that we find in Genesis is also to be found at the beginning of the Gospel of John: "In the beginning was the Word ... All things were made through him" (John 1:1, 3). John informs us that the physical universe owes its existence to God, who is the Logos. The word *logos* conveys ideas of "word," "command," and "information."

This revelation, that God by his Word imparts energy and information to create and structure the universe, is profoundly new. Yet, as I argue in detail elsewhere,[29] it converges with some of the deepest insights of a modern science that has come to realize the fundamental nature of information and its irreducibility to matter and energy.

I am therefore puzzled, to say the least, when I read John Walton's statement that "throughout the entire Bible, there is not a single instance in which God revealed to Israel a science beyond their own culture. No passage offers a scientific perspective that was not common to the Old World science of antiquity." In any case, the first sentence here seems confused. Was Israel's culture not itself shaped by God's revelation, including Genesis? The absolute nature of the second sentence ("no passage") seems to contradict Walton's own view (pointed out above) that, although there are correspondences between the Genesis cosmology and that of the surrounding nations, there are considerable differences.[30]

Walton also thinks that "we gain nothing by bringing God's revelation into accordance with today's science." I disagree. I am not, of course, claiming that the Bible can inform every branch of science, but I am claiming that there are certain fundamental points of convergence of such immense significance for our understanding of the universe and ourselves that it is worth pointing them out. Such convergences between the Bible and contemporary science add to the Bible's credibility in a sceptical world — as Scripture itself would warrant us in thinking (Rom. 1:19–20).

THE GENESIS ENIGMA

Indeed, it is interesting to see that the correspondence between the sequence given in Genesis and that given by science has been pointed out even by people who set little store on the factual accuracy of the biblical record in passages of this kind. As an example from an earlier era, English philosopher and historian Edwyn Bevan (1870–1943), in an essay titled *The Religious Value of Myths in the Old Testament*, writes,

> The stages by which the earth comes to be what it is cannot indeed be precisely fitted into the account which modern science would give of the process, but in principle they seem to anticipate the modern scientific account by a remarkable flash of inspiration, which a Christian may also call

inspiration. Supposing we could be transported backward in time to different moments in the past of our planet, we should see it first in a condition in which there was no land distinguishable from water and only a dim light coming from the invisible sun through the thick volumes of enveloping cloud: at a later moment, as the globe dried, land would have appeared; again at a later moment low forms of life, animal and vegetable, would have begun; sooner or later in the process the cloud-masses would have become so thin and broken that a creature standing on earth would see above him sun and moon and stars; at a still later moment we should see on the earth great primeval monsters; and lastly we should see the earth with its present fauna and flora, and the final product of animal evolution, Man.[31]

Much more recently, Andrew Parker, Research Director at the Natural History Museum in London, draws attention to the same phenomenon in a way that is directly relevant to Walton's view. Parker, an evolutionary biologist who does not profess to believe in God, was stimulated to look at Genesis 1 after a number of people had written to him suggesting that his research on the origin of the eye seemed to echo the statement "Let there be light." He was very surprised at what he found: "Without expecting to find anything, I discovered a whole series of parallels between the creation story on the Bible's first page and the modern, scientific account of life's history. This at least made me think. The congruence was almost exact . . ." He later adds, "The more detail is examined, the more convincing and remarkable I believe the parallels become. One question I will be asking in this book is this: could it be that the creation account on page one of Genesis was written as it is because that is how the sequence of events really happened?"[32] Here is Parker's conclusion:

Here, then, is the Genesis Enigma: The opening page of Genesis is scientifically accurate but was written long before the science was known. How did the writer of this page come to write this creation account? ... I must admit, rather nervously as a scientist averse to entertaining such an idea, that the evidence that the writer of the opening page of the Bible was divinely inspired is strong. I have never before encountered such powerful impartial evidence that the Bible is the product of divine inspiration.[33]

It is not surprising that Parker's ideas are hotly contested, particularly by atheists; but his book gives scientific support to the order of events as recorded in Genesis from someone who has no obvious axe to grind.

A PARALLEL BETWEEN COSMOLOGY AND PHYSIOLOGY?

Finally, I wish to comment further on the way in which Walton supports his view, cited above, that "the Israelites received no revelation to update or modify their 'scientific' understanding of the cosmos." He draws a parallel between cosmology and physiology, as follows:

If cosmic geography is culturally descriptive rather than revealed truth, it takes its place among many other biblical examples of culturally relative notions. For example, in the ancient world people believed that the seat of intelligence, emotion and personhood was in the internal organs, particularly the heart, but also the liver, kidneys and intestines. Many Bible translations use the English word "mind" when the Hebrew text refers to the entrails, showing the ways in which language and culture are interrelated. In modern language we still refer to the heart metaphorically as the seat of emotion. In the ancient world this was not metaphor, but physiology. Yet we must notice that when God wanted to talk to the Israelites about their intellect, emotions and will, he did not revise their ideas of physiology and feel compelled to reveal the function of the brain. Instead, he adopted the language of the culture to communicate in terms they understood.[34]

One can agree with Walton that language and culture are related, but it is the nature of that relationship which is the issue. I have already given reasons why I think that Genesis 1 is a revelation of God regarding aspects of cosmology and is not "culturally descriptive," even though it is written in language that the readers can understand and not (for very obvious reasons) in technical scientific language.

Walton claims that the biblical references to internal organs bolster his "cultural relativity" argument. He mentions several internal organs associated with intellect, emotions, and will but, interestingly, omits to mention the head in connection with dreams and thoughts (Dan. 7:1, 15).[35] He recognizes the contemporary metaphorical use of heart but claims, without giving any evidence, that in the Bible it was not metaphor but physiology. This seems very simplistic. For instance, Genesis 6:6 states, "And the LORD was sorry that he had made man on the earth, and it grieved him to his heart." I find it hard to believe that the Hebrews thought that this was a physiological statement about God. Or again, Jeremiah 23:9 says, "My heart is broken within me." Interpreted as a physiological statement, this would have to mean the physical heart pump had ceased to function.

In the ancient world, they were surely as familiar with the use of metaphor as we are. Moreover, then as now, that use was quite sophisticated. Walton mentions entrails, used to describe emotion both in the Old and New Testaments. If we ask why this term is used, surely the answer is not hard to find: the ancients, being human, noticed as we do that certain emotional states give rise to a physical feeling inside — indeed, we sometimes even nowadays call it a "gut feeling." It is a real feeling, and, by a very natural connection, the physical body part comes to stand as a metaphor for an emotional state. We should note that the use of the terms "gut feeling" and "heartfelt sympathy" does not imply that the speaker thinks that the bowels are the centre of our thought processes.

Walton continues, "The idea that people think with their hearts describes physiology in ancient terms for the communication of other matters; it is not revelation about physiology. Consequently we need not try to come up with a physiology for our times that would explain how people think with their entrails."[36]

It is a little difficult to unscramble this, since using a physical term ("heart") to communicate other matters seems to me essentially what is meant by metaphor — using something to stand for something else. Yet, unless I have misunderstood it, this interpretation contradicts what Walton has said above, that the biblical usage is not metaphor.

Furthermore, saying "it is not a revelation about physiology" is of course true in the sense that anyone can understand it, because they know the physiological reaction in the region of the heart associated with emotional thought, and they are well aware that this is what the writer is talking about and not about the blood pump in their bodies.

However, this is just where Walton's analogy breaks down, since Genesis 1, at certain points, is talking directly about cosmology. When Genesis says, "In the beginning God created the heavens and the earth," it is not using a physical piece of the universe to communicate something else at a metaphorical level: it is talking about the origin of the physical universe itself.

Walton's final statement in the above quote is, "Consequently, we need not try to come up with a physiology for our times that would explain how people think with their entrails." I am not sure what this means, since surely it is our increased understanding of physiology that gives us deeper insight into the psychosomatic relationships between thoughts, emotions, and the gut, so that we understand that there is a scientific basis to what we call "gut feeling."

Walton also comments on various aspects of design arguments. I find his discussion of the nature of the evidence for intelligent causation in the physical universe inadequate. In particular, I think that his view that "design in nature can only be established beyond reasonable doubt if all naturalistic explanations have been ruled out"[37] is false, in light of the known facts about the nature of information. But I shall not pursue this matter here since I have written about it elsewhere.[38]

Finally, I am convinced that the biblical account of *both* the material existence and function of the universe, and of human life in it, needs to be intelligently articulated in the public square more than ever before, in light of the contemporary clamour of the (now not so) New Atheists that their naturalistic understanding of the universe is the only intellectually respectable one. I find Walton's insistence that Genesis 1 has nothing to do with the material origin of the universe unconvincing for a further reason. It leaves the Bible without an account of that origin in the very place where it would be expected to occur, and where generations both of ordinary people and of scholars have thought it to be.

NOTES

1. Gordon Wenham, "Sanctuary Symbolism in the Garden of Eden Story," in *Proceedings of the Ninth World Congress of Jewish Studies* (Jerusalem: World Union of Jewish Studies, 1986), 19.
2. Rikki E. Watts, *Making Sense of Genesis 1*, Science in Christian Perspective, 2002. See http://www.asa3.org/ASA/topics/Bible-Science/6-02Watts.html.
3. John Walton, *The Lost World of Genesis One* (Downers Grove, IL: InterVarsity, 2009), 83.
4. Ibid., 96.
5. Ibid., 171.
6. Ibid., 44.
7. Ibid., 26.
8. Ibid., 43.
9. Ibid., 139.
10. See also "bara," in Brown, F., S. R. Driver, and C. A. Briggs, *A Hebrew and English Lexicon of the Old Testament* (Oxford: Clarendon, 1907).
11. Yet in many of Walton's own examples of functional creation (e.g., computers, colleges, companies, artistic masterpieces) materials are involved! "Ludicrous" appears a signally inappropriate word to use here, since, at the very least, one would have thought that it was hard to assign functional properties to something that had no material existence.
12. Walton, *Lost World of Genesis One*, 43.
13. This seems perfectly in accord with Walton's own interpretative method: "The meanings of words are established and determined by the ways in which they are used" (p. 40). Thus, though *bara* is not always used to mean "creation ex nihilo," Gen. 1:1 is surely part of the evidence that it may be understood in this way.

14. Robert Gordon, "The Week That Made the World: Reflections on the First Pages of the Bible," in McConville, J. G., and Karl Moeller, eds., *Reading the Law: Studies in Honour of Gordon J. Wenham* (London: T&T Clark, 2007).
15. Walton, *Lost World of Genesis One*, 72.
16. Interestingly, Walton does not discuss the dating of the text.
17. Walton, *Lost World of Genesis One*, 84.
18. See Collins's review at ReformedAcademic.blogspot.com, 26 November 2009.
19. Echoed in John 1:3, as referred to above.
20. Walton, *Lost World of Genesis One*, 90–91.
21. Ibid., 170.
22. Ibid., 91.
23. Ibid., 88.
24. See appendix E with reference to the Sabbath.
25. Walton, *Lost World of Genesis One*, 16.
26. See appendix C.
27. On this point see also appendix C.
28. There is an interesting parallel to this in the Memphite Egyptian cosmology, where the god Ptah creates through speech.
29. John C. Lennox, *God's Undertaker: Has Science Buried God?* (Oxford: Lion Hudson, 2009), chap. 11.
30. Walton, *Lost World of Genesis One*, 12–13.
31. Quoted in Derek Kidner, *Genesis* (Leicester, UK: Tyndale Press, 1967), 56.
32. Andrew Parker, *The Genesis Enigma* (London: Doubleday, 2009), xii–xiii.
33. Ibid., 238.
34. Walton, *Lost World of Genesis One*, 18.
35. Compare ESV "head" with NIV "mind."
36. Walton, *Lost World of Genesis One*, 19.
37. Walton, *Lost World of Genesis One*, 128.
38. Lennox, *God's Undertaker,* 135–92.

THE BEGINNING ACCORDING TO GENESIS AND SCIENCE

THOUGH, FOR THE MOST PART, Scripture is concerned with matters arguably more important than science — the why of existence, for instance, as distinct from the how of the laws and mechanisms governing the universe — nevertheless there is an important overlap. Perhaps the most important example of that overlap is the fact that both the Bible and science claim that the universe had a beginning. What is striking is that the Bible claimed it for thousands of years, whereas scientists only recently began even to entertain the possibility that there might have been a beginning. Aristotle's view, that the universe was eternal, dominated scientific thinking for hundreds of years without appreciable challenge.

Richard Dawkins was not impressed when I mentioned to him in one of our debates that the Bible was right about the universe having a beginning. He said that, since there either was a beginning or there was not, the Bible had a fifty-percent chance to get it right—no big deal. But it was a big deal. For, when scientific evidence began to indicate that the universe had not existed eternally, some leading scientists put up fierce resistance because they thought it would give too much support to those who believed in creation![1] It was not a question of guesswork. Those resisting scientific advance because they feared it supported the biblical worldview did not get their way, as the scientific evidence for a beginning proved too strong.

"In the beginning God created the heavens and the earth." These magnificent opening words of the Bible have been much studied. The definite article attached to "beginning" in the translation is missing in Hebrew. This circumstance is understood by some as having the effect of shrouding the beginning in mystery. Leon Kass, for instance, writes, "About this, too, modern cosmology cannot help but agree: 'What was there before the Big Bang?' God only knows. Despite all our sophistication, the utter mysteriousness of the *ultimate* beginning and its source or cause cannot be eradicated."[2] On the other hand, however, C. John Collins points out that "the article is missing [from the word 'beginning'] because the word is definite on its own."

Let's sit back for a moment and listen to Bill Bryson, in his inimitable style, giving a popular scientific account of the beginning:

And so, from nothing, our universe began.
In a single blinding pulse, a moment of glory much too swift

and expansive for any form of words, the singularity assumes heavenly dimensions, space beyond conception. The first lively second (a second that many cosmologists will devote lifetimes to shaving into ever-finer wafers) produces gravity and the other forces that govern physics. In less than a minute the universe is a million billion miles across and growing fast. There is a lot of heat now, 10 billion degrees of it, enough to begin the nuclear reactions that create the lighter elements — principally hydrogen and helium, with a dash (about one atom in a hundred million) of lithium. In three minutes 98% of all the matter there is or will ever be has been produced. We have a universe. It is a place of the most wondrous and gratifying possibility, and beautiful too. And it was all done in about the time it takes to make a sandwich.[3]

We take the story further, this time guided by physicist Sir John Houghton:[4]

It takes about a million years for the universe to cool enough for electrons to attach themselves to the nuclei to form atoms ... Imagine a region of higher density than the rest. The force of gravity will attract more matter into this more dense region ... Over a period of millions of years these high-density blobs will become stars and groups of stars will become galaxies ... Even more extreme conditions are generated as some stars towards the end of their lives blow themselves apart in events known as supernovae ... It is in these gigantic explosions that heavy elements such as platinum, gold, uranium and a host of others are formed.

This exploded material contains ... all ninety-two naturally occurring elements of the periodic table. In its turn it mixes with hydrogen and helium gas from the interstellar medium, to go again through the stellar evolutionary process. Second-generation stars are born ... We believe our sun to be such a second-generation star. Around our sun, planets have formed, probably as gas-and-dust clouds surrounding the young sun gradually fused together into a number of dense objects. Planet earth was born 4.5 thousand million years ago with its rich chemical composition and conditions suitable for the development of life.[5]

Houghton deduces:

For human beings to exist, it can be argued that the whole universe is needed. It needs to be old enough (and therefore large enough) for one generation of stars to have evolved and died, to produce the heavy elements, and then for there to be enough time for a second-generation star like our sun to form with its system of planets. Finally there have to be the right conditions on earth for life to develop, survive and flourish ... But that is not all. Our current understanding is that for the universe to develop in the right way, incredibly precise fine-tuning[6] has been required in its basic structure and in the conditions at the time of the Big Bang.[7]

Now the idea of a "Big Bang" is a point of concern for some people who have been influenced by Richard Dawkins's simplistic insistence on our choosing either science or God. However, these are false alternatives, on the same foolish level as insisting that we choose between Henry Ford and a car-production line to explain the origin of a Ford Galaxy.[8]

The fact is that both of these explanations are necessary: they do not contradict but complement each other. Henry Ford is the agent who designed the car; the car-production line is the mechanism by which it is manufactured. Similarly, we do not have to choose between God and the Big Bang. They are different kinds of explanation — one in terms of God's creatorial agency and the other in terms of mechanism and laws.

Furthermore, the term "Big Bang" is essentially a label put on a (fascinating) mystery. It is used by scientists to express their belief that the universe — more accurately, space-time — had a beginning. Arno Penzias, who won the Nobel Prize for Physics for discovering an echo of that beginning in the cosmic microwave background, wrote, "The best data we have ... are exactly what I would have predicted, had I nothing to go on but the five books of Moses, the Psalms and the Bible as a whole." Therefore, the Standard (Big Bang) Model developed by physicists and cosmologists can be seen as a scientific unpacking of the implications of the statement, "In the beginning God created the heavens and the earth."[9] There is a certain irony here, in that the very same Big Bang cosmological model of the universe that confirms the biblical claim that there was a beginning also implies that the universe is very old.

It is worth reminding ourselves that scientific confirmation of the initial creation event is the kind of thing that the apostle Paul would lead us to expect (Rom. 1:19–20). God has left his fingerprints in creation: natural theology is a legitimate exercise. That is why I have drawn attention to the current convergence between science and the biblical record on the beginning of space-time.

NOTES

1. One notable such scientist was John Maddox, the then editor of the scholarly journal *Nature*.
2. Leon Kass, *The Beginning of Wisdom* (Chicago: University of Chicago Press, 2006), footnote on 28.
3. Bill Bryson, *A Short History of Nearly Everything* (London: Black Swan, 2004), 28.

4. Former professor of physics at Oxford, then head of the UK Meteorological Office, and subsequently chairman of the Nobel Prize–winning Intergovernmental Panel on Climate Change (IPCC).

5. John Houghton, *The Search for God: Can Science Help?* (Oxford: Lion, 1995), 27–28.

6. For examples of this fine-tuning, see above, under John C. Lennox, *God's Undertaker: Has Science Buried God?* (Oxford: Lion Hudson, 2009), 31–46. (This is the chapter on "The Scope and Limits of Science.")

7. Houghton, *Search for God*, 33–34.

8. For more detailed explanation, see John C. Lennox, *God's Undertaker: Has Science Buried God?* (Oxford: Lion Hudson, 2009), 45.

9. Concerning "heavens and earth," see footnote in chap. 5, under "God Is the Eternal Creator."

TWO ACCOUNTS OF CREATION?

AN ARGUMENT that is frequently advanced against allowing a significant chronological dimension in the early chapters of Genesis is that the creation account given in Genesis 2 contradicts any chronology based on Genesis 1. One point at issue is that chapter 1 describes the creation of the plants before that of humans, whereas Genesis 2 seems to give the reverse impression. Here is the relevant text from Genesis 2 as given in ESV:

> When no bush of the field was yet in the land and no small plant of the field had yet sprung up—for the LORD God had not caused it to rain on the land, and there was no man to work the ground, and a mist was going up from the land and was watering the whole face of the ground—then the LORD God formed the man of dust from the ground and breathed into his nostrils the breath of life, and the man became a living creature. And the LORD God planted a garden in Eden, in the east, and there he put the man whom he had formed. And out of the ground the LORD God made to spring up

every tree that is pleasant to the sight and good for food. (Gen. 2:5–9)

C. John Collins points out that the ESV rendering of the Hebrew *ha'arets* as "land" rather than "earth" in the first of these verses is preferable, since the lack of plants here is not put down to the fact that they had not yet been created but that there was no rain. In light of that, Collins deduces that the scenario depicted here would be a very familiar one to the readers. They would understand "a land in which the rain falls during the winter and not at all during the summer. This weather pattern makes the ground quite dry and brown by the end of the summer and the coming of the rains brings about plant growth. The only way to overcome this natural pattern is for man to work the ground, by irrigation in this case."[1]

In other words, Collins suggests that the Genesis 2 account has nothing to do with the original creation of plant life on day 3, but rather is saying that at a particular time of the yearly cycle in a particular land, before the plants had started to grow, God created human beings.[2] Now this reading of the text clearly assumes that the cycle of nature has been established long enough for it to be relevant, so that, in order to harmonise it with the events of day 6, one must conclude, as Collins points out, either that the creation days of Genesis 1 are not (all) ordinary, or that they are separated in time. He regards the first of these two options as preferable, viewing the days as God's workdays, so that how long they are does not affect the act of communication. In chapter 3 of this book I advance some arguments for the second option or a variant of it, although it is clear that the effective difference between the two is small.

Another suggestion that has been made is that the order in the first creation account is principally chronological, whereas in the second it is principally logical. Indeed, in ordinary speech and writing, we often mix logical order with chronological order without necessarily being aware of it. Jim bought a car. He drove it home. You ask where he keeps it. Well, he built a garage to put it in. He built the garage when he brought it home? No, the garage was actually already there. That fact could have been made clearer in English by using the pluperfect tense "he had built," rather than using the simple past tense, "he built."

Hebrew does not have a separate pluperfect tense, with the result that precise chronological sequence is not always as immediately clear in Hebrew as it would be in English. For this reason, some argue that the order of events in Genesis 2:5–9 clashes with that of Genesis 1 only if we assume that both orders are of the same type. However, the matter is resolved if the first account is predominantly chronological, describing the sweep of creation from its beginning to its goal, the creation of human beings, whereas the second account places man at the centre and gives a predominantly logical account of the meaning of what it means to be human, a circumstance that not all translations make clear.[3] However, it must be said that the use of the word "when" in Genesis 2:5 might well support Collins's interpretation.

Hebrew has, however, ways of expressing a pluperfect sense that help to solve another apparent chronological clash between Genesis 1 and 2. Some translations of Genesis 2:19 suggest that the creation of animals took place after that of man. For example, "Out of the ground the LORD God formed every beast of the field and every bird of the heavens and brought them to the man to see what he would call them" (ESV). Collins argues that the Hebrew verb should be translated by the pluperfect "had formed" (see ESV margin), thus obviating the chronological clash.[4]

NOTES

1. C. John Collins, *Genesis 1–4: A Linguistic, Literary, and Theological Commentary* (Phillipsburg, NJ: P&R, 2006), 126.

2. A (major) variant of this view is that of John Sailhamer, *Genesis Unbound* (Sisters, OR: Multnomah Books, 1996). He holds that Gen. 1:1 describes the period of the creation of the universe and Gen. 1:2–2:4a describes a one-week period (in the usual sense) during which a particular land, the promised land, was prepared and human beings created in it.

3. The NIV uses the pluperfect English tense to bring out the sense. For more detailed comments on the use of the pluperfect, see the essay by Alistair McKitterick, "The Language of Genesis," in Norman Nevin, ed., *Should Christians Embrace Evolution?* (Nottingham, UK: Inter-Varsity, 2009), and the references given there. However, it should be noted that Robert Gordon holds that introducing the pluperfect only gives partial and superficial relief to the perceived tension between the narratives of Gen. 1 and Gen. 2 (see "The Week That Made the World: Reflections on the First Pages of the Bible," in McConville, J. G., and Karl Moeller, eds., *Reading the Law: Studies in Honour of Gordon J. Wenham* [London: T&T Clark, 2007]).

4. C. John Collins, "The Wayyiqtol as 'Pluperfect': When and Why?" *Tyndale Bulletin* 46, no. 1 (1995): 117–40.

APPENDIX E

THEISTIC EVOLUTION AND THE GOD OF THE GAPS

ACCORDING TO GENESIS 1 the sequence of creation acts came to an end. On the seventh day God rested. The work of creation was done. That would seem to imply that what went on during the creation sequence is no longer happening, an implication that has consequences for one of the major assumptions of science — the uniformity of nature, the idea that the present holds the key to the past, at least to within a minute fraction of a second from the beginning.

Putting it another way, Genesis seems to be saying that nature has not been absolutely uniform. Genesis is not denying the important fact that nature is *largely* uniform. Indeed, a further implication of the Sabbath is that, after his creation activity, God continues to sustain the universe. The universe constantly depends on his providential care,[1] which means we can rely on the regularities of nature that God himself built in at the beginning. A famous example of this is contained in a statement of Jesus: "For he makes his sun rise on the evil and on the good, and sends rain on the just and on the unjust" (Matt. 5:45). Christianity, therefore, is not to be equated with deism, which holds that God lit the fuse triggering the origin of the universe and then retired from the scene and had no further involvement. On the other hand, the very concept of the Sabbath implies that God's providence in maintaining the universe in existence does not exhaust what the Bible means by *creation*.

The New Testament confirms these two aspects of God's relationship to the universe as both Creator and Sustainer. Paul ascribes these two functions to Christ: "For by him all things were created"; and, "In him all things hold together" (Col. 1:16, 17). Similarly, the letter to the Hebrews says of Christ, "through whom also he created the world"; and, "he upholds the universe by the word of his power" (Heb. 1:2, 3).

According to Genesis, then, creation involved not just one, but a sequence of several discrete creation acts,[2] after which God rested. This surely implies that those acts involved processes that are not going on at the moment. Of course, such (supernatural) creation acts ("from above") would appear to science ("from below") as discontinuities or singularities, a suggestion that is highly unpalatable to scientists in general and biologists in particular.

For example, physicist Paul Davies, whom we referred to earlier,[3] writes (from a nontheistic perspective),

> Ascribing the origin of life to a divine miracle not only is anathema to scientists but also is theologically suspect. The term 'God of the gaps' was coined to deride the notion that God can be invoked as an explanation whenever scientists

have gaps in their understanding. The trouble with invoking God in this way is that, as science advances, the gaps close, and God gets progressively squeezed out of the story of nature. Theologians long ago accepted that they would forever be fighting a rearguard battle if they tried to challenge science on its own ground. Using the formation of life to prove the existence of God is a tactic that risks instant demolition, should someone succeed in making life in a test tube.[4] And the idea that God acts in fits and starts, moving atoms around on odd occasions in competition with natural forces, is a decidedly uninspiring image of the Grand Architect.[5]

Many scientists who believe in God think, similarly, that the idea of God interfering or, less pejoratively, intervening at intervals is a kind of semideism and is unworthy of God. They hold that nature possesses "functional integrity," in the sense that life is the fruitful outworking, according to the God-given laws of nature, of the potential built into the capabilities of matter by God at the beginning without the need for further discrete intervention. Surely, a theistic evolution[6] of this kind, they say, is more worthy of God than millions of different supernatural acts of creation to produce the vast array of species—even though there is no suggestion (in Genesis or by me) that there were millions of separate creation acts. After all, the number of occurrences of the phrase "And God said ..." is very small.[7]

Eminent biologist Francis Collins describes his understanding of theistic evolution as follows:

> I found this elegant evidence of the relatedness of all living things an occasion of awe, and came to see this as the master plan of the same Almighty who caused the universe to come into being and set its physical parameters just precisely right to allow the creation of stars, planets, heavy elements, and

life itself. Without knowing its name at the time, I settled comfortably into a synthesis generally referred to as 'theistic evolution,' a position I find enormously satisfying to this day.[8]

Collins goes on to flesh out his position:

> God, who is not limited in space and time, created the universe and established natural laws that govern it. Seeking to populate this otherwise sterile universe with living creatures, God chose the elegant mechanism of evolution to create microbes, plants and animals of all sorts. Most remarkably, God intentionally chose the same mechanism to give rise to special creatures who would have intelligence, a knowledge of right and wrong, free will and a desire to appreciate him.[9]

However, Collins explains, there came a point in history where God specially conferred his image on a creature that had emerged from the evolutionary process. This was the beginning of the human race "made in the image of God."[10]

The main points of this version of theistic evolution would appear to be as follows:

1. God causes the universe to come into being.
2. God sets the laws of physics and the fine-tuned initial conditions.
3. God sustains the universe in being.
4. The universe develops and life subsequently emerges without any more special discrete supernatural input from God, until God creates human beings.
5. At a particular moment, God specially conferred his image on a hominid that had already emerged from the gradual evolutionary process.[11]

There are other versions of theistic evolution. For instance, one variant denies 5, claiming that 4 includes the emergence of human beings.

Biochemist Michael Behe accepts 1, 2, and 3, but not 4. He believes that evolution has occurred in the Darwinian sense, but that it has been "supervised." He argues that the scientific picture is that natural selection and *random* mutation do something, but that their reach is relatively limited: there is an "edge" or limit to evolution's variational capacity that can be transcended only if mutations are introduced that are *nonrandom*. In other words, Behe is suggesting that an input of intelligence is needed and that a designer[12] got involved in these mutations. Thus, on this view, God moved atoms on many occasions in the evolutionary process.

In this connection, it seems to me that the C. S. Lewis – Francis Collins version of theistic evolution also involves moving atoms, since it is very hard to imagine, granted our current insights into the brain and its functioning, how God could impart his image on a pre-existing creature without fundamental adjustments to the neural system in the brain to create the necessary physical substrate to carry this new dimension of God-consciousness.

Cambridge paleo-biologist Simon Conway Morris gives a further variant of theistic evolution. He suggests that the uncanny ability of evolution to find its way through the space of all possible paths to what he calls "life's solution" is congruent with creation: "For some it will remain as the pointless activity of the Blind Watchmaker, but others may prefer to take off their dark glasses. The choice is yours."[13]

Now all of this has the salutary effect of forcing me to think very hard. First of all, I am not a biologist (though I try hard to follow what they write), and secondly, and more importantly, I have the greatest respect and admiration for these people and their stand against atheism. In particular, Francis Collins has been a great encouragement to me personally. However, I still wish to add my pennyworth to the discussion.

As a scientist I am sensitive to the danger of falling into a "God of the gaps" mentality and running the risk of intellectual laziness. For that reason I hasten to say that I do not find the main evidence for God's activity in the current gaps in the scientific picture. I see evidence of God everywhere in the science we do know — indeed, I see it in the very fact that we can do science. I agree wholeheartedly with Francis Collins that God created the natural laws that govern the universe. God is the God of the whole show. Indeed, for me as a mathematician the very mathematical intelligibility of the universe, and the subtlety and power of the mathematics developed to describe it, constitute major evidences for the existence of a Creator.

I go further. I also agree that God is the cause of the universe's coming into being, and that God fine-tuned its physical parameters and set its initial boundary conditions so that the formation of the elements and (at least two[14]) generations of stars occurred that ultimately gave rise to planets endowed with the heavy elements that are necessary for life.

Where I begin to have problems with theistic evolution[15] is at the next stage. So far we have been thinking not about biology but about cosmology, physics, and chemistry. As a result of a process inaugurated and supervised by God and covered by the known laws of physics, which were designed by God, we have arrived at a world which possesses the raw materials of life.

Theistic evolution now asks why we should introduce a special supernatural act of creation at the point of the origin of life. Would it not be more consistent, says theistic evolution, to think that the origin and development of life proceeded in exactly the same way as the processes before the origin of life? Surely it would be a pity, having come so far, now to introduce a God (of the Gaps) simply because there is, as yet, no plausible explanation for the origin of life? This last point is rather ironic, because by it theistic evolutionists open themselves up to the very same charge over the origin of the universe and, in many cases, the origin of human life.

Of course, the issue is not whether or not God could have done it in a particular way. Clearly, as a basic principle, God, being God, can do it any way he chooses. And he has, so far as we can see, chosen to do *part* of it by using what we often call "natural processes" — like the formation of galaxies, suns, and planets. The question is, did God do it *all* in that way? Is there any reason to think that there were several discrete acts of creation (e.g., origin of life, humans) within the history of the universe that are fundamentally different from events that normally happen in God's world governed by his laws?

And why does it matter anyway? Is this not a case of Christians getting involved in an irrelevant sideshow? I do not think so, especially in light of the current insistence on the part of many atheists that there is nothing special about human beings, since they have been produced by precisely the same blind and unguided process as any other species. The status of human beings is no small matter.

SINGULARITIES, MIRACLES, AND THE SUPERNATURAL

Three considerations weigh with me at this juncture. Firstly, it is common knowledge that most physicists seem to be able to live with the view that the origin of space-time is a singularity. Certainly, theistic evolutionists seem comfortable with the idea that God was responsible for that singularity as Creator—he was the First Cause. The universe did not come to be through natural processes. The reason something exists rather than nothing is that God willed it to be so.

Secondly, as we pointed out earlier, many theistic evolutionists hold that the origin of human life involved some kind of supernatural discontinuity.

Thirdly, and most importantly, it is part of the historic Christian faith that there have been other singularities in more recent history—preeminently the incarnation and resurrection of Jesus Christ. These events have a physical dimension, but they clearly do not fall within the range of the explanatory power of the laws of nature. On the contrary, these events were caused, as the New Testament indicates, by the direct input of divine power from outside. Yet those of us who are Christians believe that these events actually occurred, even though many of our atheist scientific colleagues (erroneously) protest that the laws of nature forbid such occurrences.[16]

That being the case, I find it strange that some Christians seem to find a priori difficulty in the claim that there have been some additional singularities in the past, like the origin of life and the origin of human beings. Surely, if one grants, say, at least three major singularities — creation, the incarnation, and the resurrection — there can be no in-principle objection to believing in (a relatively few) more singularities, especially if there is both scientific and biblical evidence to support them.

The question arises whether we are to think of the singularities involved in creation as miracles. For instance, biologist Denis Alexander writes:

> In biblical thought the language of miracles seems to be generally reserved for those special and unusual workings of God in his *created order* and in the lives of his people. This does not exclude the possibility that God performs particular miracles during his *work of creation*, but if that is the case then Scripture is silent about that aspect of his *creative work*. When Jesus intervenes to turn water into wine, or calm a rough sea, or raise Lazarus from the dead, these miraculous signs stand out as such because they are so different from God's normal way of working in *creation*.
>
> Science is based on observed regularities and logical induction to unobserved regularities. The secular scientist assumes that everything works in a regular, reproducible kind of way because that is what science has always found to be the case so far. The scientist who is a Christian agrees, but in addition believes in a logical basis for that order, the *creator* God who faithfully endows the universe with its regularities. There is something paradoxical about the suggestion that miracles can be regular or even predictable events in God's *general work of creation*. The whole point about miracles is that they are unexpected, irregular events, particular signs of God's grace; so my suggestion is that Christians use the language of miracles with the biblical understanding in mind.[17]

We note that Alexander uses the word "creation" both to describe the original act of creation at which God endowed the universe with its regularities and to describe the product of that act, the creation that now exists and whose regularities are studied by scientists. These regularities are understood to be part of what Alexander calls "God's general work of creation," presumably referring to God's continuing to hold the universe with its regularities in existence — the "present tense" of creation as he calls it.[18] These are distinctions I readily accept, if I have understood him correctly.

For us to be able to recognise "miracle," in the New Testament sense of "wonder" or "sign," as C. S. Lewis pointed out, the universe must exhibit regularities that are known. Otherwise, as Alexander says, Jesus' miracles would not "stand out." However, such miracles, as Lewis went on to argue, do not "break" the regularities enshrined in the laws of nature. It is rather that God (the Lawgiver) feeds a new event into the system by his divine power. It is an exceptional, as distinct from a normal, act of God.[19]

Since the miracles of the Bible are recognised as such because they stand out against the known regularities of the universe, the term *miracle* would scarcely be strictly appropriate for the initial creation of the universe with those regularities. However, this does not mean that the initial creation did not involve a number of direct interventions by God in order to *set up* the universe with its regularities. The word *supernatural* would therefore be more appropriate. Alexander seems to miss this distinction. After all, the statement "In the beginning was the Word ... all things were made through him" (John 1:1, 3) does not use the language of miracle, although supernatural activity of the highest order was clearly involved.

It follows that, although the word *miracle* is not used,

the Bible is not silent on the fact that God's *supernatural* activity was involved at creation. Indeed, that seems to be the whole point of the creation sequence—to differentiate, *within* the period from the absolute beginning to the flowering of human civilisation, between God's special creation acts and his providence (or general work in creation, to use Alexander's phrase) in holding the universe in being in the intervals between those acts and subsequently.

It is failure to distinguish the miraculous from the supernatural that leads Alexander to make what seems a very strange statement: "There is something paradoxical about the suggestion that miracles can be regular or even predictable events in God's general work of creation." No one, as far as I am aware, would think of saying that miracles are regular or predictable events.[20] What I am suggesting is that both the direct supernatural action of God and his providence were involved during the creation period.[21]

Finally, I think that Alexander's assertion that science has so far *always* found that *everything* works in a regular, reproducible kind of way does not hold.[22]

In theological terms, theistic evolution seems to adopt an essentially Augustinian view of creation as ultimate causation. That is, *creation* expresses the idea of the dependency of the universe on God: God causes the universe and its laws to exist and endows it with its potential.[23] Such dependency is, of course, a fundamental aspect of creation, but I do not think that this is all that is implied by the biblical use of the term *creation*. For, in both Old and New Testaments, the Bible clearly distinguishes between God's initial acts of creation on the one hand and his subsequent upholding of the universe on the other. This distinction is also apparent in Genesis 1: it records a sequence of creation acts followed by God's resting. I also think, by contrast with my theistic evolutionary friends, that science supports this distinction.

ARE ALL GAPS BAD?

That brings us back to the matter of gaps. There would appear to be different kinds of gap, as I have argued in detail elsewhere.[24] Some gaps are gaps of ignorance and are eventually closed by increased scientific knowledge — they are the bad gaps that figure in the expression "God of the gaps." But there are other gaps, gaps that are *revealed* by advancing science (good gaps). The fact that the information on a printed page is not within the explanatory power of physics and chemistry is not a gap of ignorance; it is a gap that has to do with the nature of writing, and we know how to fill it — with the input of intelligence.

As we have seen — so forgive me if I labour the point — physicists and cosmologists have become accustomed to the idea that their mathematical model of the origin and expansion of space-time leads them to conclude that there is a singularity or gap at that origin where the laws of physics break down. Most Christians readily accept that the ultimate explanation of that singularity, and of the laws of nature, is God. That means that they accept that, although God can act indirectly, there must be some point or points at which he acts directly. Causing the universe to exist in the first place was surely one such direct action of God.[25]

In this connection, one of the things I find striking is that, after stating that God created the heavens and the earth,[26] the creation narrative, as I understand it, passes over vast stretches of time (and much physical and chemical activity) with no comment whatsoever until we arrive at a formless and empty earth. It is at that point that Genesis 1:2 tells us, "The Spirit of God was hovering over the face of the waters."

Astrophysicist Hugh Ross suggests that this statement gives us a frame of reference and point of view just above the surface of the earth in a specific place.[27] This, incidentally, may well provide an answer to the question, if most of Genesis 1 is concerned with global phenomena — the heavens, earth, land, sea, sky, and so on — why does it talk about day and night, even though night and day occur simultaneously on different sides of the earth?[28]

More than that, reference to the Spirit of God hovering near earth could be understood as a dramatic indication that God's special action is now going to begin. The aeons of waiting are over. The Creator is about to shape his world, to create life and fill the earth with it in preparation for God's crowning final act, the making of man and woman in his image.

That impression of special action is strongly confirmed in the biblical account of the origin of life. On day three we are told that God spoke more than once. First, God separates the dry land and the sea. Then God speaks again: "And God said, 'Let the earth sprout vegetation ...'" (Gen. 1:11). In other words, according to Genesis, you do not get from inorganic matter to organic by unguided natural processes.[29] Life does not emerge from nonlife without God having to get directly involved and speak his word.[30]

The question is, does science give any evidence for such singularities? My answer is that, just as science and the Bible converge and complement each other on the origin of the universe, so do they on the origin of life.

First, we must clear away a major potential misunderstanding. Contrary to widespread public impression, (neo-) Darwinian evolution cannot account for the *origin* of life. Richard Dawkins was simply wrong when he said in *The Blind Watchmaker* that natural selection explained not only the variation in life but also the *existence* of life. His error has nothing to do with belief in God but is a simple matter of logic. Darwinian evolution *presupposes* the existence of a mutating replicator in order to get going in the first place. Hence Darwinian evolution, by definition, cannot be an explanation for the *existence* of the very thing without which it itself cannot get started. This obvious fact was recognized long ago by the famous Russian biologist Theodosius Dobzhansky, who said, "Prebiological evolution is a contradiction in terms."[31]

It is good to see that, in his much more recent book *The Greatest Show on Earth*,[32] Dawkins admits that natural selection cannot explain the existence of life. However, he goes on to say something very odd: "We don't actually need a plausible theory of the origin of life, and we might even be a bit anxious if a too plausible theory were to be discovered!" His argument is that if there were a plausible theory, then life should be common in the galaxy. But what has the commonness of life in the galaxy to do with the *plausibility* of a theory of life's origin? A plausible theory might well confine the likelihood of life existing to earth. In fact, a plausible theory of the origin of life does exist: that God created it on a planet he had specially prepared for that purpose.

What Dawkins may mean is that if there were a plausible *naturalistic* theory showing that, where the physical and chemical conditions were such and such, life was more or less bound to occur, then we would, on statistical grounds, expect there to be quite a lot of life out there. But there isn't such a theory.

A MATTER OF INFORMATION

The catch is that the nature of life itself militates strongly against there ever being a purely *naturalistic* theory of life's origin. There is an immense gulf between the non-living and the living that is a matter of kind, not simply of degree. It is like the gulf between the raw materials paper and ink, on the one hand, and the finished product of paper with writing on it, on the other. Raw materials do not self-organise into linguistic structures. Such structures are not "emergent" phenomena, in the sense that they do not appear without intelligent input.

Any adequate explanation for the existence of the DNA-coded database and for the prodigious information storage and processing capabilities of the living cell must involve a source of information that transcends the basic physical and chemical materials out of which the cell is constructed. As Microsoft founder Bill Gates has put it: "DNA is like a computer program, but far, far more advanced than any software we've ever created."[33] Such processors and programmes, on the basis of all we know from computer science, cannot be explained, even in principle, without the involvement of a mind.

Amir Aczel, a mathematician, writes, "Having seen how DNA stores and manipulates tremendous amounts of information ... and uses this information to control life, we are left with one big question: what created DNA ... was it perhaps the power, thinking and will of a supreme being that created this self-replicating basis of all life?"[34] The answer is surely, yes.

Unguided natural processes do not generate language-type information found in RNA and DNA.[35] Indeed, even if unguided natural processes were to produce a machine (which assumption is of course essential to atheistic belief), that machine would still not create any novel information. Léon Brillouin, in his classic work on information theory, writes: "A machine does not create any new information, but it performs a very valuable transformation of known information."[36]

What I find odd about the (theistic) evolutionary view of the origin of life is that it seems to fly in the face of these scientific considerations. I fail to see evidence that the God-given laws of nature, working on the matter he created, starting with initial conditions set by him, are adequate to ensure that the universe and life will "emerge" without any special, discrete, supernatural input. Mathematical laws of the type that are familiar to us from physics are just not adequate to do the job, for the simple reason that they cannot create information.

Paul Davies asks: "Can specific randomness be the guaranteed product of a deterministic, mechanical, law-like process, like a primordial soup left to the mercy of familiar laws of physics and chemistry? No it couldn't. No known law could achieve this—a fact of the deepest significance."[37]

And yet the claim is that such processes not only created information but also created a creature that could create information. Surely not! Scientific considerations from information theory point in the exact opposite direction, straight towards a special, intelligent, creative act as the only credible solution to the question of the origin of life's biological information.[38]

This contrasts sharply with a remark made by Denis Alexander on the origin of life: "Imagine going into an artist's studio ... and then telling the artist 'you've chosen the wrong type of paints, they're really hopeless!' I think we would all agree that would be insulting. But to confidently proclaim that the precious materials which God has brought into being in the dying moments of stars do not have the potentiality to bring about life seems to me equally insulting."[39]

This argument is fatally flawed, since the analogy does not correspond to the application. No one is suggesting that the Creator's materials are "the wrong type" or "hopeless." What is being suggested is that the Creator's good materials cannot bring life into existence without the additional direct intelligent input of the Creator. This is no more an insult to the Creator than it would be an insult to the artist to suggest that his paints are incapable of producing a masterpiece without his direct input. It is rather the (ludicrous) suggestion that the paints could do it on their own without him that would be an insult to the painter!

Furthermore, it is no more intellectual laziness to reject the idea that life is a product of the latent potential of matter and energy working according to the laws of nature than it is intellectually lazy to abandon the search for perpetual motion, or to attribute a magnificent painting to the creative genius of Leonardo da Vinci rather than to the latent physical and chemical capacities of paint and canvas.

And that brings us back to Paul Davies's assertion that "the idea that God acts in fits and starts, moving atoms around on odd occasions in competition with natural forces, is a decidedly uninspiring image of the Grand Architect." First, the idea that the God who invented natural forces could be in competition with them sounds self-contradictory. What, then, about the business of God moving atoms? Leonardo da Vinci can also help us here. Neither the mind nor information is a material substance. Yet the conceptual information in Leonardo's mind moved the atoms in his hand that moved the atoms of the paintbrush that moved the atoms of paint that produced his masterpieces. None of those movements was in *competition* with natural forces. On the contrary, they *involved* natural forces directed by mind. Now, God is Spirit, and not material. And, since God moved atoms (or rather created them) to launch the universe, since he moved atoms to raise Jesus from the dead, it follows that Davies has got it completely wrong. It would be an "uninspiring image" of the Creator *not* to credit him with moving atoms at the origin of life and at the creation of his masterpiece—human beings made in his image in such a way that their minds could move atoms too.

COMMON ANCESTRY?

The idea of a special creation of human beings will be challenged by the following evolutionary argument. Human beings and animals share many common features in terms of large-scale structures of bones and organs, down to the similarities in their genetic material. These features imply that there is a seamless evolution, by natural unguided processes, up through the forms of life from primitive to complex. Although there are gaps in the fossil record, there is nevertheless a fairly universal consensus among biologists that the details will eventually be filled in. They regard the molecular evidence for the evolutionary interrelatedness of all life as essentially conclusive.

The similarities are undeniable, of course. But similarities can be a result of design as distinct from descent; or, indeed, from a combination of the two, as selective breeding demonstrates. Therefore, an evolutionary explanation of the similarities in terms of natural selection only carries authority insofar as there is evidence that the suggested evolutionary mechanisms can bear the weight that is put on them. As I argue elsewhere,[40] they can clearly bear some weight, but whether they can bear the weight of the difference between animals and humans is another matter. And it is a quantum difference. Geneticist Steve Jones writes, "A chimp may share 98% of its DNA with ourselves but it is not 98% human: it is not human at all—it is a chimp. And does the fact that we have genes in common with a mouse or a banana, say anything about human nature? Some claim that genes will tell us what we really are. The idea is absurd."[41]

In his book *The Music of Life: Biology beyond the Genome*, systems biologist Denis Noble explains in more detail how tiny differences in genome sequence can encode enormously complex differences in function. However, Noble also points out, regarding the genome (and, indeed, the brain), that "we need to recognise that these are databases that the system as a whole uses. They are not programs that determine the behaviour of the system."[42] Intriguingly, Noble likens the human genome, with its roughly thirty thousand genes, to an immense organ with thirty thousand pipes (there are such): "The music is an integrated activity of the organ. It is not just a series of notes. But the music itself is not created by the organ. The organ is not a program that writes, for example, the Bach fugues. Bach did that. And it requires an accomplished organist to make the organ perform." Noble then asks: "If there is an organ, and some music, who is the player and who was the composer? And is there a conductor?"[43] Excellent questions. Whether Noble has answered them satisfactorily is another matter, but the very fact that he is asking them is a heartening change from the extreme reductionism that has characterised much of the writing on this issue.

Biologists Jerry Fodor and Massimo Piattelli-Palmarini, though not doubting that evolution has occurred, are deeply concerned about the "distressingly uncritical" nature of "much of the vast neo-Darwinian literature," and concerned that "the methodological scepticism that characterises most areas of scientific discourse seems strikingly absent when Darwinism is the topic." This, according to them, applies particularly to the role played by natural selection.

> Natural selection has shown insidious imperialistic tendencies. The offering of post-hoc explanations of phenotypic traits by reference to their hypothetical effects on fitness in their hypothetical environments of selection has spread from evolutionary theory to a host of other traditional disciplines: philosophy, psychology, anthropology, sociology and even to aesthetics and theology. Some people really do think that natural selection is a universal acid, and that nothing can resist its powers of dissolution.
>
> However, the internal evidence to back this imperialistic selectionism strikes us as very thin. Its credibility depends largely on the reflected glamour of natural selection which

biology proper is said to legitimise. Accordingly, if natural selection disappears from biology, its offshoots in other fields are likely to disappear as well. This is an outcome much to be desired since, more often than not, these offshoots have proved to be not just post hoc but ad hoc, crude, reductionist, scientistic rather than scientific, shamelessly self-congratulatory, and so wanting in detail that they are bound to accommodate the data. So it really does matter whether natural selection is true.[44]

In our context, one of the most interesting statements by Jerry Fodor comes in an earlier article:

In fact an appreciable number of perfectly reasonable biologists are coming to think that the theory of natural selection can no longer be taken for granted ... The present worry is that the explication of natural selection by appeal to selective breeding is seriously misleading, and that it thoroughly misled Darwin. Because *breeders have minds* (italics added), there's a fact of the matter about what traits they breed for; if you want to know, just ask them. That strains the analogy between natural selection and breeding, perhaps to the breaking point. What, then, is the intended interpretation when one speaks of natural selection? The answer is wide open as of this writing.[45]

Unsurprisingly, Fodor has provoked a storm.

And he is not the only one raising questions about natural selection. Biologist William Provine, in a remarkable afterword published in a new edition of a classic work, explains that his views have "changed dramatically": "Natural selection does not act on anything, nor does it select (for, or against), force, maximize, create, modify, shape, operate, drive, favour, maintain, push or adjust. Natural selection does nothing. Natural selection as a natural force belongs in the insubstantial category already populated by the Necker/ Stahl phlogiston or Newton's 'ether' ... Having natural selection select is nifty because it excuses the necessity of talking about the actual causation of natural selection. Such talk was excusable for Charles Darwin, but inexcusable for Darwinists now. Creationists have discovered our empty 'natural selection' language, and the 'actions' of natural selection make huge vulnerable targets."[46]

More recently biologist Robert G. Reid has added to the question marks over natural selection in his comprehensive work *Biological Emergences: Evolution by Natural Experiment*,[47] of which a reviewer, Christopher Rose, wrote, "Reid argues convincingly that the selectionist paradigm is a conceptual dead end for understanding innovation since it mistakenly views natural selection as a creative force in evolution."[48] Reid is well aware of the risks of his undertaking: "Since neo-Darwinists are also hypersensitive to creationism, they treat any criticism of the current paradigm as a breach of the scientific worldview that will admit the fundamentalist hordes. Consequently, questions about how selection theory can claim to be the all-sufficient explanation of evolution go unanswered or ignored."[49] He then details substantial evidence that natural selection cannot bear the weight that is often put upon it.

It would now seem that Richard Dawkins's concession (of the obvious fact) that natural selection does not account for the origin of life is far from adequate: natural selection would appear to account for very little at all in the development of life.

This does not of course mean that the scientists quoted above have given up on the naturalist paradigm. It does mean, though, that there is a shift away from simplistic reductionism to "emergentist" explanations that raise even more sharply the question of the input of information from an intelligent source and make the a priori exclusion of such input appear all the more arbitrary. For "emergence" is turning out to be another slippery term that can mask a number of hidden assumptions.[50]

Welcoming Reid's book, the reviewer interestingly concludes,

> On the upside, evolutionary biology needs to be pushed beyond reductionist/gene-centric explanations for properties like multicellularity, body plans, behavioural flexibility, self-maintenance, homology and human intelligence. The important events in life's history clearly involved causal factors at numerous levels of organisation, none of which have inherent priority over the others. On the downside, emergentism will undoubtedly increase the challenges of teaching evolution theory and convincing the public (and ourselves) that biologists know what we are talking about.[51]

EVOLUTION OF THE GAPS?

Although the charge of believing in a God of the gaps must be taken seriously—it is, after all, possible for a theist to be intellectually lazy and say, in effect, "I can't explain it, therefore God did it"—it is important to say that sauce for the goose is sauce for the gander. Many of those who accuse Christians of God-of-the-gaps thinking are themselves guilty of the very same thing. For instance, Paul Davies, who, as we saw above, does not believe that known law can create the information necessary for life, therefore invokes unknown natural law as his gap filler.

Evolution is also a notorious gap filler. It is not hard to cobble up a speculative just-so story and say that "evolution did it." Indeed, a scientist of naturalist convictions *has* to say that natural processes were solely responsible for the existence of life and all of its various forms, since there is no admissible alternative in the naturalistic worldview.

Nobel laureate physicist Robert Laughlin, whose research is on the properties of matter that make life possible, issued the following warning to scientists about the dangers of this kind of thinking:

> Much of present day biological knowledge is ideological. A key symptom of ideological thinking is the explanation that it has no implications and cannot be tested. I call such logical dead ends anti-theories because they have exactly the opposite effect of real theories: they stop thinking rather than stimulate it. Evolution by natural selection, for instance, which Darwin conceived as a great theory has lately come to function as an anti-theory called upon to cover up embarrassing experimental shortcomings and legitimize findings that are at best questionable and at worst not even wrong. Your protein defies the laws of mass action — evolution did it! Your complicated mess of chemical reactions turns into a chicken — evolution! The human brain works on logical principles no computer can emulate? Evolution is the cause![52]

I suspect that belief in an evolution of the gaps is probably more widespread than belief in a God of the gaps, since concentration on the latter allows the former to thrive undetected.

Tempted as I am to explore this matter further, I must leave it here with a thought experiment about descent and design. Suppose that scientists manage one day to produce life in the laboratory from nonliving chemicals — as many believe they will, in light of Craig Venter's construction of a synthetic bacterium using a genome contained in a computer programme. Suppose, further, that this life thrives and establishes itself as a new species, Species X, say. Now imagine that all scientific records of this are lost, and in the far distant future scientists come across Species X. If neo-Darwinism is still the reigning paradigm, these scientists will inevitably argue that Species X is related to all other life by an uninterrupted naturalistic evolutionary process. They will be wrong, will they not? The relationship of Species X to other species involves a special and discrete input of information by intelligence. What is more, that intervention of human intelligence is, by definition, invisible to neo-Darwinism — just as invisible as is the special creation of humans by God to neo-Darwinism today. But neo-Darwinism is not the only pair of glasses on the market.

NOTES

1. See, for example, Job 38–39 and Psalm 104.
2. This is not to be thought of as a form of semideism. Semideism would teach that God did a series of creative acts but was not involved in the subsequent maintenance of the universe.
3. See chap. 5, under "God Is Distinct from His Creation" and "God Has a Goal in Creation."
4. This assertion is plainly false. What the making of life in a test tube by a scientist would show is that mind acting on matter could produce life — which is precisely what Christians claim that God actually did.
5. Paul Davies, "E.T. and God," *Atlantic Monthly*, September 2003, See http://www.theatlantic.com/past/docs/issues/2003/09/davies.htm.
6. Theistic evolution is sometimes called "evolutionary creationism" (Alexander) or "biologos" (Francis Collins).

7. We should also note that, in any case, it would be rash to equate the word translated "kind" in Genesis 1 with our modern term "species." The term "type" might be more appropriate as a translation.

8. Francis Collins, *The Language of God* (New York: Free Press, 2006), 199.

9. Ibid., 200–201.

10. This view seems also to have been that of C. S. Lewis, although his scepticism about the adequacy of the evolutionary account appears to have grown over the years. See "Is Theology Poetry?" in *They Asked for a Paper* (London: Geoffrey Bles, 1962), chap. 9. See also Gary B. Ferngren and Ronald L. Numbers, "C. S. Lewis on Creation and Evolution: The Acworth Letters, 1944–1960," *PSCF* 48 (March 1996): 28–33; available at www.asa3.org/aSA/PSCF/1996/PSCF3–96Ferngren.html.

11. We note that this looks very much like a special "intervention" by God.

12. Behe is at pains not to identify the designer, in order not to confuse the science with the theology.

13. Simon Conway Morris, *Life's Solution* (Cambridge: Cambridge University Press, 2005), 329–30.

14. Needed for the production of the necessary heavy elements.

15. The word "evolution" in the phrase "theistic evolution" tends to cover more than biological evolution. The prebiotic phase has, however, nothing to do with evolution in the sense of (neo-)Darwinism, which, of course, presupposes by definition that life already exists.

16. This common objection is essentially that of David Hume, and I address it in John C. Lennox, *God's Undertaker: Has Science Buried God?* (Oxford: Lion Hudson, 2009), chap. 12.

17. Denis Alexander, *Creation or Evolution: Do We Have to Choose?* (Oxford: Monarch, 2008), 38.

18. Ibid., 31.

19. See my detailed discussion of this in *God's Undertaker*, chap. 12.

20. Although we should not forget that Christ's resurrection was predicted.

21. For an excellent account of the God's relationship to his creation, see C. John Collins, *The God of Miracles* (Wheaton: Crossway, 2000).

22. See Lennox, *God's Undertaker*, chap. 7. Of course if science is *defined* as the study of reproducible regularities then the assertion is tautologous. But the whole history of the universe is not reproducible, so that science, thus defined, could have nothing to say about that!

23. For a comprehensive contemporary exposition of the Augustinian view in relation to modern science, see Alister McGrath's Gifford Lectures 2009, published as *A Fine-Tuned Universe* (Louisville: Westminster John Knox Press, 2009).

24. Lennox, *God's Undertaker*, 188–92.

25. That is one of the reasons why I think I am, in principle, no more a God-of-the-gaps man than C. S. Lewis or Francis Collins is when he assigns the gulf between animals and human beings to God's special conferment of his image.

26. We might just note that the heavens come before the earth—cosmology says the same, of course.

27. Hugh Ross, *The Genesis Question* (Colorado Springs: Navpress, 2001), 21.

28. In connection with the idea of perspective from a time, rather than a spatial, point of view, it has been suggested that we need to take factor in Einstein's famous discovery that time is relative when attempting to understand the nature of the days of Gen. 1. See Gerald Schroeder, *Genesis and the Big Bang* (New York: Bantam, 1990).

29. See *God's Undertaker*, chaps. 9–11.

30. No detail is given of what precise processes are subsumed under the statement, "Let the earth bring forth." The crucial thing is that it did not happen without the direct activity of the word of God. This is another instance of "all things were made through him" (John 1:3).

31. Theodosius Dobzhansky, *The Origins of Prebiological Systems and of Their Molecular Matrices*, ed. S. W. Fox, (New York: Academic Press, 1965), 310.

32. Richard Dawkins, *The Greatest Show on Earth* (London: Free Press, 2009), 421.

33. Bill Gates, *The Road Ahead* (Boulder, CO: Blue Penguin, 1996), 228.

34. Amir Aczel, *Probability 1: Why There Must Be Intelligent Life in the Universe* (New York: Harvest, 1988), 88.

35. The order arising from self-organisation scenarios is in a different category. See Lennox, *God's Undertaker*, 129ff.
36. Léon Brillouin, *Science and Information Theory* (New York: Academic Press, 1962).
37. Paul Davies, *The Fifth Miracle* (London: Penguin, 1998), 89. "Specific randomness" is a technical concept used in connection with information.
38. For more detail on this central issue, see Lennox, *God's Undertaker*, and also Stephen Meyer, *Signature in the Cell* (New York: HarperCollins, 2009).
39. Alexander, *Creation or Evolution*, 333.
40. *God's Undertaker*, chap. 6.
41. Steve Jones, *The Language of the Genes* (London: HarperCollins, 2000), 35. See also Lennox, *God's Undertaker*, 141, for some amplification of this point.
42. Denis Noble, *The Music of Life: Biology beyond the Genome* (Oxford: Oxford University Press, 2006), 130.
43. Ibid., 32.
44. Jerry Fodor and Massimo Piattelli-Palmarini, "Survival of the Fittest Theory," *New Scientist*, 6 February 2010, 28–31. A fuller account is given in their book, *What Darwin Got Wrong* (London: Profile, 2010).
45. Jerry Fodor, "Why Pigs Don't Have Wings," *London Review of Books*, 18 October 2007, 20, 29.
46. William B. Provine, *The Origins of Theoretical Population Genetics* (Chicago: University of Chicago Press, 2001), 199–200.
47. Robert G. Reid, *Biological Emergences: Evolution by Natural Experiment* (Cambridge, MA: MIT Press, 2007).
48. Christopher Rose, review of *Biological Emergences: Evolution by Natural Experiment* by Robert G. Reid, in *Integrative and Comparative Biology* 48, no. 6 (2008): 871–73.
49. Reid, *Biological Emergences*, 2.
50. See Lennox, *God's Undertaker*, 55–56.
51. Rose, op. cit., 871–73.
52. Robert Laughlin, *A Different Universe: Reinventing Physics from the Bottom Down* (New York: Basic Books, 2005), 168–69.

ACKNOWLEDGMENTS

I HAVE BENEFITTED over the years from interactions with many people and from reading many books and commentaries, but I am chiefly indebted to my lifelong friend and mentor Professor David Gooding, Member of the Royal Irish Academy. It was he who first drew my attention many years ago to the fact that Genesis 1 is concerned not simply with creation, but also with organization. I also owe to him innumerable insights into the riches of the Bible that have influenced me so profoundly that they have become an intrinsic part of my thinking. I would like to thank Barbara Hamilton for her invaluable help in spotting grammatical and stylistic infelicities in my original manuscript. I am also indebted to my research assistant, Simon Wenham, for his constant, cheerful input and critical eye.

GENERAL INDEX